Praise for *Celebrate High School*

Having a copy of *Celebrate High School* is akin to having a comforting friend who knows the path ahead and shows me where and when to plant my very unsure "homeschooling in high school" feet.

Penni
Mom of 2015 home education graduate accepted at her first-choice university

Celebrate High School is my go-to-guide for all things related to high school. Cheryl's book is filled with invaluable information from writing course descriptions, awarding high school credits, creating transcripts, and my favorite, making a four-year plan. *Celebrate High School* is easy to follow and empowers parents who are on this unique homeschool journey. As a parent of both a middle schooler and a high schooler, I reference this book throughout the year.

Massiel
A homeschooling mom of middle and high school young adults

I found your organizational tips invaluable, especially as they relate to cumulative record keeping. Thank you, Cheryl, for sharing your wisdom with the homeschooling community.

Lisa
Mom of a 2015 homeschool graduate

Celebrate High School gave me confidence to navigate high school. The ideas kept me organized in my record keeping and prepared me for important deadlines. Sections I found invaluable included writing course descriptions and creating transcripts, using the four-year plan worksheet, keeping reading lists, and documenting credit hours. The Bright Futures information was also helpful. In a panic, before my daughter entered ninth grade, I bought every book I found that addressed homeschooling high school. *Celebrate High School* was the only one I consistently used all four years. I look forward to the updated version as my son enters his high school years.

Sarah
Mom of a 2014 homeschool graduate

Our daughter was accepted to Stetson University beginning fall 2015. She will be receiving the Faculty Scholarship for academic excellence award—$25,000 for next year! This honor would not have been possible without your help guiding me through the process. It was and is very appreciated by our family!

Stephanie
Mom of a 2015 Florida home education graduate

Celebrate High School was indispensable! I cannot thank you enough for writing it. Without your book and transcript help, I could not have finished well. Cheryl, your input on our daughter's transcript was absolutely remarkable, as well as professional. Her transcript, book list, and course descriptions were received well and she was accepted at each one of the colleges to which she applied! She was offered generous academic and athletic scholarships. Although, there was opportunity for her to play for Division 2 schools, she chose to attend a Division 3 college where she accepted academic scholarships to continue a Christian education and play on the women's basketball team. We believe none of this would be possible without your book. Bless you for helping her dreams come true!

Barb
Mom who turned her seventh, and final, homeschool tassel May 2015

Entering high school at home was an easy transition for us thanks to Cheryl's book, *Celebrate High School*. Easy step-by-step instructions for developing a four-year plan, writing course descriptions, understanding graduation requirements, and creating transcripts made this resource invaluable. With this book, Cheryl's many hours of research and experience is right at your fingertips.

Amie
Mom of a 2014 homeschool graduate and current high school student

Celebrate High School covers many important details about how to successfully navigate homeschooling through the middle and high school years. I appreciated the easy-to-read format as well as the wisdom *Celebrate High School* imparted, offering our family freedom in selecting courses that allow our children to develop their strengths while building competitive transcripts.

Lucee
Florida mom of middle and high school students

Celebrate High School has helped me tremendously! The book helped me learn how to organize records, format my son's transcript, and write course descriptions. Cheryl's book gave me the knowledge I needed to tackle all of our high school years. It has been the go-to-reference I refer to often. I highly recommend this book to anyone thinking about home schooling through high school. It has all the needed resources to finish successfully!

Michele
A homeschooling mom

Celebrate High School
Finish with Excellence

Cheryl A. Bastian

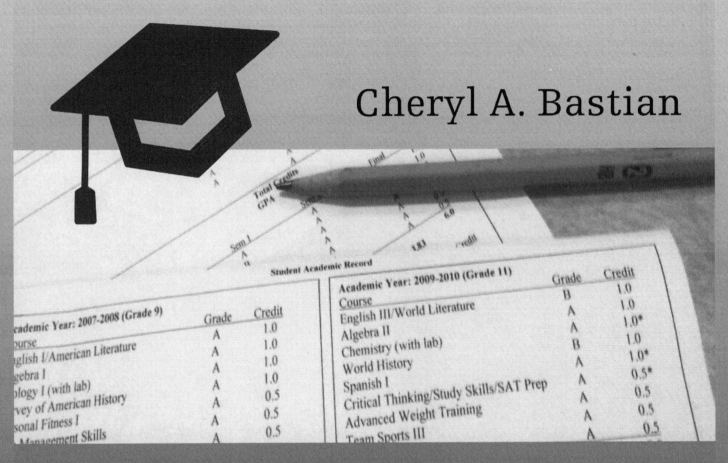

A guide to middle & high school home education

CELEBRATE
SIMPLE

Celebrate High School: Finish with Excellence

Front cover photography: Eve Bastian
Back cover photography: Eve Bastian
Cover design: John and Kimberly Drake and Evan Travelstead

ISBN 978-0-692-48597-2

Zoe Learning Essentials

Inquiries regarding speaking engagements or ordering information should be addressed to the author's attention at:

Cheryl@cherylbastian.com

Additional resources are available at:

www.cherylbastian.com
and
www.cherylbastian.blogspot.com

Foreword

I like to ask questions. Questions invite people into conversation and the answers, surprising as they may be, offer another perspective or profound truth. Curiosity breeds questions and questions foster curiosity.

This week I started a conversation with my teens at the dinner table. Our dialogue continued about five minutes at which time my four-year-old chimed in, "What you're really saying is that we should love God and love others." I was amazed. I asked a question and, though not directed toward my four-year-old, she had been listening to the conversation and understanding every point. A child can teach us profound truths.

My daughter's comment reminded me of a time when I was astounded by another answer from one of my children. While on Christmas break twenty-three years ago, I purposed to spend the first couple days of my vacation playing with my oldest son. We did. Eventually, I told him that I had to do some planning for the semester. After a few questions and dialogue, he looked at me and responded, "No, you must play with me. I am your work." I then asked what my school work was and he answered, "That is your hobby." Some parents might say this was a disrespectful response; however his poignant answers and insight changed my view of work. My son was right; family relationships are my greatest work.

How are these stories related to a high school journey? Curiosity does not have to end with the inquisitive preschool years. Questions, and their answers, aid young adults in finding out who they are. Our family has experienced the rich rewards of productive conversations even when they did not go as planned. In fact, some of the outcomes changed the trajectory of the lives of our young adults. Children of all ages need willing teammates, people who listen and help them process as they navigate their interests and possible career fields.

When I was young, beginning to make independent decisions, yet too inexperienced to see the possibilities and consequences of my actions, I needed someone to listen—who was not quick to judge—in order to process my thoughts and ideas. I needed a teammate who had resources and a driver's license so I could try some of my adventures, a teammate who wouldn't do things for me, but who would give me the dignity to attempt and accomplish my goals. I needed my parents more than I could express or even admit—parents who were willing to stretch and think outside their predetermined box for me.

Asking questions and walking alongside looks different for every child and parent; each must be willing to walk their journey together. To team up with my middle and high schoolers, I had to be curious about them. When I was truly interested in them, not just my ideas about them, they knew it. Together, we opened up to one another and discovered the interests and strengths God created in them, as well as how those gifts might be used, not just in high school, but in life. And, that, my friend, is an opportunity worth celebrating!

Mike Bastian

Contents

Contents

Acknowledgements

Let's celebrate! I've come to the end of my journey with this book, just as you will end a similar journey when your young adult graduates from high school.

I have to be honest; the last three weeks have been difficult. There were late nights of coffee-induced writing frenzies to make deadlines—and I don't normally drink coffee. Other days I wanted to give up. Many were the days when baby lay across my lap while I worked, smiling at me one minute, spitting up on me the next. And, there were meals to cook and emails to answer. Oh, yeah, and weave in hosting annual homeschool evaluations too.

I remember similar days and nights during my son's senior year hurrying to upload documents to university inboxes, just barely meeting admission deadlines. However, the end results of both journeys are timeless, eternal, and worth every effort—because people's lives matter.

I'm often asked how I "do it all." Well, I don't. Without my incredibly supportive and gracious husband, Mike, I could not do what I do. He is a willing servant—washing dishes, taking children to the park, changing diapers, and listening to my endless ideas. I'm thankful for his wisdom and insight, and feel tremendously blessed to walk alongside him through life. We really are a team.

My children inspire me! Through their play, they discover. Through life, they learn. Their exuberance reminds me to "Celebrate Simple," for it's through the simple—those caterpillars emerging and that ant carrying a leaf—that we learn the profound. My children bring joy to my day, reminding me of what's truly important. It is an absolute delight to explore, discover, and find solutions together.

When you turn the tassel for your graduate, there will be people who contributed behind the scenes, imparting truth to your young adult in profound ways. In fact, they may not even know the enormity of their influence. The publication of this book is similar. Some of the most instrumental people were the ones who worked behind the scenes, and unless I introduced them to you, their efforts would go unnoticed. I can't let that happen. They're just too important to me and their efforts to help will influence you, the reader.

When I think of books, I think of Tina Farewell. Tina's *Always Incomplete Guide Resource Guide and Catalog* blessed me before I met her. When we met, our conversations were engaging and my educational philosophy was turned upside down. A great influencer in my life and the home education book industry, her wisdom and insight in regards to the format revision of this book were valuable. In addition, I appreciated her prayer support and encouragement.

Julie Mayhew, a faithful mom and friend of almost twenty years, answered my frantic prayer and email for editing help, offering excellent advice and corrections in her typical quiet and gentle manner. Even after forty pages of rough text, she politely asked if there was anything else she could do. Amazing!

Then, there are our dear friends John and Kimberly Drake. They offered, selflessly in the middle of their family dinner, to digitize my thoughts, creating the first cover sketches. I shared my ideas and then played with their boys while they worked. Kimberly persevered with me until the final PDF was sent to the printer.

John and Kimberly introduced me to Evan Travelstead who drafted new logos under a tight deadline and completed his creative work at our kitchen table with my high schoolers watching, intrigued. He not only created our logo, but shared his enthusiasm for graphic design.

We learn together and from one another. Therefore, I invited moms to share their family's stories of the middle and high school years, knowing their experiences would encourage you. I gratefully accepted personal narratives from Connie Albers, Lisa Beach, Sherry Boswell, Denise Carr, Cindy Floyd, Fran Haig, Penni Holt, Amie Hurley, Sarah Margheim, Julie Mayhew, Shannon McLaughlin, Renee Nix, Anita Robinson, Dawn Strobeck, Kym Valk, Faith Whittingham, plus several moms who contributed anonymously. Special thanks to Lisa Beach who kindly offered her graduate's transcript as a guide for other parents.

Planning a celebration—a milestone—is a team effort. Every person plays a unique role, contributing their talents, time, and energy to the culminating event. Surely, no celebration—birth, graduation, marriage, employment—occurs without the support and encouragement of significant individuals. Likewise, putting *Celebrate High School* into print required a devoted, strong network. I am grateful for the team that surrounded me.

I often encourage parents in my workshops with these words, "Where God calls, He provides." Whether writing a book or mentoring a young adult through high school graduation, God is faithful and He *does* provide! Let's rejoice in His provision together, celebrating the high school journey and finishing, together—with excellence.

Dear Fellow Homeschool Parent,

Last week I read a story. My mind painted pictures as the story jumped off the pages, begging me to read more. As I did, the story invited me to meet the characters—to join them on their journeys. I understood the challenges they faced and felt the excitement of their accomplishments. The story was well-penned by an author who loved his work.

Your home educated high school student has stories too. They tell about their character, talents, and education through their resumes, transcripts, course descriptions, reading lists, letters of recommendation, community service hours, and co-curricular activities. Employers and college admission personnel who read the students' stories come to know the main characters—the students—while reading the details of his or her important documents. Each student's unique story is priceless. But, just how do parents write their student's stories?

Getting stories on paper is not as daunting as it seems. In fact, many parents, though hesitant at first, have persevered and successfully navigated the record keeping and writing path. They tell their stories in this book.

My husband Mike and I do consultations and annual evaluations for many families. As we sit around the table together, students share their work samples and tell us about their extraordinary learning adventures and parents ask questions. *Celebrate High School* answers their most commonly asked questions about writing transcripts, keeping records, and gaining admission to universities or military academies.

This book is not meant to be an exhaustive wade-through-all-the-chapters-to-find-what-you-need resource, but, instead it is a quick, easy-to-read reference, a catalyst for your own personal research. Designed to encourage and equip parents, this revised edition includes narratives from parents who have celebrated high school with their young adults and who want to help you experience that joy!

Whether you are writing the first sentence of the preface or you are editing the final manuscript, your student's story is significant and valuable. My hope is that I can help you chronicle his or her high school journey so that at the turning of the tassel you can *celebrate high school and finish with excellence!*

Cheryl

The information in this book occasionally references requirements for students in Florida. As a Florida resident, this is the information with which I am most familiar. I am not familiar with the home education laws of all fifty states. High school is not a one-size-fits-all experience, therefore no resource can encompass all the necessary information for every student, in every state. Become your student's advocate and best resource and, in turn, you will tell their unique story, well.

Chapter 1

Magnificent, Make-A-Difference Middle School

Summer. A mother and two sons, three or four years apart in age, sit on a riverbank in Dayton, Ohio. The boys fish, with little success. Mother watches nearby, enjoying the boys, eager to answer questions. A bird swoops, plunging its long sparring beak below the water's surface, spearing a fish then soaring off into the sky. The boys study every second, intrigued by the bird's graceful, yet purposeful flight. Mesmerized, the oldest boy turns to Mother asking, "What makes a bird fly?"

Father's gift, a rubber band-propelled helicopter, intrigues them. Fueled by curiosity and ingenious minds, the boys set up a work space and collaborate for hours each day. Each contributes to the wonder, to the solving of problems. A desire to win a sled race motivates them to modify the runners sending the sled soaring down the hill. Faces feel the wind; Mother explains wind resistance. Success.

Visiting the junk man, they learn people nearby have spare parts they may be able to use or sell. A wagon would help them collect their treasures. Agreeing they need a light-weight, sturdy wagon to carry heavy wheels and metal pieces, they get to work, building. Mother insists they draw projects first so the finished products turn out as planned. Sandpaper, tape measures, rulers, pencils, and paper are available to them at home. Demonstrating responsibility, the boys are allowed to use Dad's tools.

Their wagon adventure is trial and error but brings success and teaches the boys about friction. The boys continue building and experimenting. Their passion for flight, for learning, grows. They also read, read every book they can find—many from their extensive home library.

They seek for mentors, for people versed in their fields of interest, from the man at the junk yard to experienced aviators and businessmen. When they can not afford parts, they make them. Their quest—bigger than themselves—brings mistakes, adversity, and even controversy, but they press forward. What began on riverbanks, two boys intrigued by flight and a mother eager to answer questions, eventually takes off at the Outer Banks and impacts the world.

Celebrating High School Begins in Middle School

The Wright brother's younger years were ripe with curiosity, imagination, and ingenuity. Given opportunities to develop strengths and interests, their experiences set the stage for future decisions, decisions that moved them forward. In the middle school years, home educated students have the ability to study what intrigues them, what makes them curious. On these pursuits they learn thoroughly, deeply, developing and building a large working vocabulary, and explore possible career fields--all which may better light the pathway from the middle school years into the high school years.

The middle school years are an opportune time to continue fostering interests. They are also years to begin investing in opportunities which involve others, perhaps community and volunteer service, team sports, and youth leadership. Responsibility, work ethic, life and communication skills are inherent to these outside, extracurricular experiences. These experiences help middle schoolers reach out to something bigger, something that touches the heart, something that impacts the lives of others, something much more gratifying than social and digital media. When there are not significant opportunities for contribution and service, doors open for wasting time and defaulting to status quo.

Coaching Your Middle Schooler

Wilbur and Orville Wright needed coaches and cheerleaders. Susan Wright, their mother, was their greatest cheerleader, accompanying them on lakeside picnics to observe birds and being available to listen to their ideas and answer their questions.

In our family, Mike and I teamed up with our young adults during their middle school years. What a joy to watch them grow. The process reminds me of a butterfly emerging from a chrysalis, spreading fresh wings to fly. With each successive middle schooler, we learned to parent better. For example, with our first middle schooler, we were more directors than coaches. As we learned from our mistakes and applied coaching techniques our relationships improved and our children felt more confident in their strengths as they moved toward independence.

Middle schoolers need cheerleaders: people to cheer them on, answer their questions, affirm their successes, and come alongside when ideas fail. Like adults, middle schoolers gravitate toward sources of encouragement and affirmation. Our experience is that they will hang out most—physically and emotionally—with those who encourage and affirm best.

Consequently, we purposed to be the coaches and cheerleaders in our middle schoolers' lives. Yes, there were times when we had "to be the parents," but honestly, those times became fewer and further between as our middle schoolers knew they had the ability to make wise decisions and carry out their ideas. When they understood what responsibility was and that they could act responsibly, they made mature decisions, eventually becoming mature, independent young adults.

Communication became an important component to coaching and cheering our middle schoolers—and remains today as we affirm our adult children. When we processed hard situations, unfortunate circumstances, and even everyday occurrences, we tried—and were not always perfect—to create an environment free of sarcasm or critical comments. If these elements entered the conversation or discussion we apologized and asked for forgiveness as quickly as possible. Misunderstandings did occur, just as they do with adults who share feelings about sensitive issues. Again, we tried to clear up any miscommunication at the first available opportunity.

We also learned that being independent does not mean being "like you". Our middle schoolers—and now adults—do not make the same decisions we would in any given situation. Though their decisions may not be the same as ours, they are still reasonable. Interestingly, we have learned from watching and listening to our adult children as much as they have learned from us. I am grateful our children taught us that lesson.

Susan Wright *knew* her boys and she enjoyed helping them pursuit their interests. She spent countless hours teaching them, listening to ideas, and hearing their concerns. She *knew* their strengths, provided the means by which they learned best, and helped them to see how they could help each other achieve their dreams.

Before I can help my children understand themselves, I must *know* them. To *know* my children, I have to spend time with them, observing, listening, and asking. I watch how they act and respond in both stressful and rewarding circumstances. I observe what activities they enjoy and what makes them smile. Body language and verbal responses are windows to their hearts. What they read expresses their interests. Who my children talk about gives me understanding into the character they emulate and respect. *Knowing* our children takes diligence and purpose, but is deserving of my time and energy. When I come to *know* my children—what motivates, intrigues, and captivates them—I can begin to help them understand themselves.

Middle school students often need honest, gentle insight as they learn who they are, where or by what means they learn best, what skills they have or want to attain, and how they can contribute to their homes, neighborhood, church, city, and eventually state, nation and world. Asking the right types of open-ended questions will help them uncover the answers. Middle schoolers may need help processing in an environment free of condemnation. In fact, we have found if our children feel like they have to give a "right" answer to questions such as those listed below, then the "right" answer will be given, which defeats the purpose of gaining insight.

- What are my interests?
- What are my strengths?
- How do I learn best?
- Where do I learn best?
- Do I need quiet to study?
- Will white noise or classical music help me concentrate?
- Can I learn this independently or will I need guidance?
- What subjects do I need to study early in the day?
- Would I learn this material better if it were in another format, perhaps an audio book, e-reader, commentary, or theater presentation?
- Do I need to turn off my phone when studying?
- Where do I like to serve?

On a personal note, my middle school years were difficult, awkward, and sometimes very frustrating. There were days I did not feel anyone understood my thoughts or feelings, if I had the confidence to share them. I have noticed the same to be true of our middle school learners. There are awkward days, days where confidence is beyond reach. Emotions are triggered quickly and in a moments notice, nothing is right. These are times when an understanding, sensitive, encouraging adult or sibling helps to set the world right—maybe. As I reflect on my middle school years, I am reminded that as a parent of young adults, I must be ready to turn off dinner, set aside the cell phone, and sit down on the couch to listen. If I do not take time, feelings and emotions remain tense, confusing, and misunderstood.

Once our middle school students gained a better understanding about their physical, emotional, and spiritual changes as well as how they could use their strengths to contribute, their moods evened out and they were more purposeful in the coming and goings of their days. We did not get to the destination over night. The journey took countless conversations, a multitude of trial and error opportunities, and mutual respect. The end results were well worth the effort.

Help Me Make A Difference

Wilbur and Orville Wright knew if they put man in flight their accomplishment could change history. Granted, they may not have envisioned changing history as middle schoolers, but as their interest and knowledge grew, they began to understand the magnitude of their work.

In the same way, middle schoolers need time and experiences to help them understand who they are and what they can contribute to their community, nation, and the world. They need something to ponder, practice, and pursue, a way to make a difference. Making a difference, they feel the satisfaction of collaborating and contributing, serving and giving.

Parents can help middle schoolers by calling out strengths and interests, asking questions, processing feelings and ideas, and navigating difficult situations and relationships. Affirming statements sprinkled throughout the day empower middle schoolers giving them significance and confidence. For example, thanking your middle schooler student for using mechanical skills to help a neighbor fix a lawn mower not only brings attention to the skills the student has, but also provides a verbal reward for the positive use of time and energy. We have discovered the combination of a positive experience, an intrinsic feeling of satisfaction for service, and an acknowledgement of the effort sets a foundation stone in the building of understanding and character.

When our middle school students come to us with an idea, a solution to a problem, or a project they want to start, we do our best to sit, listen, and encourage. As the child talks, we listen for ways we can foster the interest and walk alongside the process. We are careful not to change the idea or step in and solve problems, but do offer resources if needed. By asking questions we help the middle schooler think and come to conclusions.

When there is failure, we encourage a retry. Once middle schoolers know they can make a difference, a new world opens. They realize making a difference takes time. Having time to investigate their interests, use their strengths, and make a difference requires good time management skills.

A Reason to Celebrate

My boys were early language users. Before they could write, I stapled together sheets of colored paper and took dictation. They would play with toys, roll around on the ground, and wonder about while telling me a story. I wrote every word, and they illustrated the story.

When I realized their inability to write was slowing down the storytelling process, I introduced Storybook Weaver *software. My sons choose characters from a menu and created their own stories using a keyboard instead of pen or pencil. As writing skills improved, the stories became more elaborate. I believed that my children might have a talent as storytellers, and I became a steward of honing that skill.*

At an early age, we gave them a cheap video camera. My three-year-old began by filming and running a commentary of everything he filmed. Looking back, we realize we offered them the tools that they needed to develop their God-given skill as storytellers. The camera built a passion for making movies. During those years, I was never the director. Instead, I was told where to place lights, what props were needed—swords and shields were essential. I was also the costume designer (no sew) and required to attend every performance.

As the boys got older, I introduced them to stop motion animation. I found a curriculum on movie production and introduced them to great writing. Even better I offered them great audio books. The Narnia series and Chuck Black's Kingdom Series have been, and still are, listened to over and over again.

Today my boys attend public high school. They still love to write and make movies. This year, between the two boys, they earned five awards for film group projects at the district level. My youngest had one film advance to regionals and state competition. Their friends are fellow movie makers. A sleepover at our home involves groups of boys filming, making props, and editing—and eating lots of food.

As a homeschool parent, I was anxious about getting the core subjects taught. Now I look back and realize I gave my boys a great gift. I gave them time to develop a love for making movies. I am not sure how God is going to use their gifts.

Though I worried, the academics got done. My children read at a college level, assimilated into public school well, and excel academically. My satisfaction is not so much their academic achievement, but that they had the time to develop what have become clear strengths and talent, and an opportunity for them to continue to bond together as brothers.

Help Me Manage Time

The Wright brothers' interest in physics and flight kept them engaged. The more bicycle wheels and mechanical parts they found in the junk, the more they worked. The wind resistance they felt flying down the hill on their sled motivated them to build more creations. As their creations gathered speed, so did their momentum to learn more. To build, they needed time and an ordering of priorities to achieve their goal—put man into flight.

Several facets of life motivate middle schoolers to manage their time: knowing they have skills to solve a problem bigger than themselves, having a project to complete or a problem to solve, and understanding they can use their skills to contribute to a cause. When these aspects are discovered and fostered, managing time matters. If there is more to accomplish than there is time, time management is a necessity.

When our children hit the middle school years they had many aspirations. Two wanted to start businesses. A Boy Scout fixed his eyes on Eagle rank. Two played travel baseball. One played the violin. Another read. Three enjoyed art. They knew if they completed school work before lunch, they could pursue other interests in the afternoons. Using their time wisely was the key to accomplishing their goals.

My husband encouraged our children to use a spreadsheet, similar to the one on page 17, to analyze their use of time. We discussed priorities—appointments, classes, deadlines, practices, and special events—and why these items should be placed on the schedule first. Eating, exercise, and personal care were considered priorities and added. After priorities, they logged less significant tasks and events. Their completed spreadsheets provided a visual representation of how and where they were spending time. This tool helped our students plan and manage their days. Did they mismanage time? Yes, especially when they first started planning. We encouraged them to keep trying, reminding them adults sometimes make poor choices, too.

A spreadsheet is only one time management tool. Your student may prefer a single page weekly schedule, a digital application, or a spiral bound planner. If one method is not effective, try another. A young adult who is comfortable with a method will be more likely to use it efficiently.

We helped our young adults look for wasted or dead time. For example, our daughter had an extensive vegetable, flower, and herb garden. Every morning she would head outside to water her plants, standing while allowing water to flow from the hose. After talking with her about her goals, she determined standing to water was dead time and decided to wear a cooking apron while watering so she could put her Kindle in the front pocket. Wearing earphones, she watered and listened to *Anne of Green Gables*. Amazed at her ingenuity I affirmed her creativity, learning from her in the process.

Part of being a good time manager is being organized so time is not wasted on extra steps or errands. For middle schoolers to be successful at managing their time they must learn to be organized, to put all the essentials for one task in one place where it can be found or returned when not in use. Placement of tools and resources offers opportunities for conversation and problem solving.

Help Me Organize

Reverend Wright, the father of Orville and Wilbur, allowed the boys access to his workshop and tools. Susan Wright insisted the boys draw their creations before building as not to waste time measuring and cutting incorrectly. Keeping workspace and thoughts organized helped Wilbur and Orville learn and create efficiently.

Middle schoolers are not usually naturally organized. They may need us to brainstorm ideas. They may need us to take them to the store to purchase organizers. Organization is another key to success, for adults of all ages.

Big projects will require big space, whether a desk, workbench, or corner of the yard. Small projects may require a notebook or small countertop organizers. When a middle schooler shares a project, ask how he or she will organize the finances, supplies, resources, or tools. He or she may welcome help to plan, prepare, and order a work area.

Case in point, when my daughter started her bow business, she envisioned shelves mounted to her bedroom wall to store spools of ribbon. She had an idea to ask her grandfather, a carpenter, for his ideas about making a spool shelf. Their time together was special. He was helping her solve a problem; she was learning from his skill and craft. The shelf was made, painted, and hung, keeping the spools from unraveling and tangling. Her desk was organized

Weekly Planning Log

	Monday	Tuesday	Wednesday	Thursday	Friday	Saturday	Sunday
6:00 am							
7:00 am							
8:00 am							
9:00 am							
10:00 am							
11:00 am							
Noon							
1:00 pm							
2:00 pm							
3:00 pm							
4:00 pm							
5:00 pm							
6:00 pm							
7:00 pm							
8:00 pm							
9:00 pm							
10:00 pm							

- Log everything you do during the week. Include specific course study, sports, even eating.

- List below activities which you would like to schedule.

_____

_____

_____

_____

- Is there anything in the schedule which could be deleted and replaced with a more important activity?

- Schedule the activities above as time allows.

with a holder for her ruler, scissors, and glue gun. The work area she created was efficient and neat—unless she was working on a large order. Having a special space in her room allowed her to work freely without me nagging her about frayed ends on the living room carpet.

Another of our middle schoolers had an idea—build a marble run. Her plan was to create a descending maze of cardboard tubes through which a marble would run and land in an open cup fastened at the end of the long tunnel. The tubes, she envisioned, would be taped to a closet door. Enthused, eyes full of confidence; she asked if we would help collect paper towel and toilet paper rolls. We agreed to help, cheering her efforts, though I have to admit I was not thrilled about toilet paper tubes being taped to the closet door.

Tubes began to appear everywhere, under her bed, in the closet, on the kitchen counter. I began to get annoyed. I could either lose my patience or help her find a storage solution. Choosing the solution option, we decided a box in the closet would be best. For three weeks, the pile grew. Finally the day arrived when she felt she had collected a sufficient supply for her endeavor. With tape in hand, she built and built. By the end of the afternoon, with many trials and a few errors, the announcement was made. "Mom, come here! Look at this!"

Finding a solution to storing paper tubes was paramount to the success of the marble run creation project. Our daughter needed help collecting the tubes, but she also needed us to be patient and find a storage solution. Without our team work, our daughter would have never experienced the exhilaration of accomplishing her quest—to build a marble run the height of a doorway.

Help Me Find Resources

The Wright brothers obtained resources. They requested use of Father's tools and knew the junkyard man could help them find parts. Mother furnished paper, pencil, anything she had around the property. Even better, she showed them by example how to live and solve problems. Resources were necessary and knowing where to find them proved essential to their eventual success.

Middle schoolers have ideas and interests they want to pursue. There are things they want to build, books they want to write, businesses they want to start, logos they want to design, and fish they want to catch. Resources, tools, and significant people put those ideas and interests in motion.

Budding entrepreneurs, writers, artists, inventors, programmers, and scientists need tools. These items may be helpful to our middle school students as they discover, create, and invent:

- Three-ring binder with subject tab separators
- Plastic sleeve protectors
- Notebooks or notebook paper
- Construction paper
- Receipt books or accounting softward
- Pencils, mechanical or wooden according to child's preference
- Ruler, architect triangular scale ruler, and protractor
- Stapler
- Tape dispenser with refills
- Bookcase
- Microscope

- Digital camera
- Photo editing software or applications
- Laptop, notebook, or I-pad with office-related software
- Wood scraps
- Cloth and fabric remnants
- Art supplies
- Compass and navigation applications
- Cardboard
- Duct tape
- Special cooking, baking, or candy making equipment and tools

One of the greatest resources is time—time to process, think, and talk through ideas. In conversation and through experience, middle schoolers learn to plan, design, analyze, and evaluate, all which work together for understanding. Without time, these key life skills cannot develop. Fleshing out thoughts, finding solutions, and learning from mistakes--middle school students love discovery, but need time to do so.

I allow time, margin in the day, for our middle schoolers to dig into areas of interest. One middle schooler wanted to write every day to add to in a historical fiction memoir. Another needed two hours a day to build inventory for an upcoming craft event. Both worthy goals, attainable because I allowed them time to pursue their goals. Not only did they accomplish their goals, but I was able to add creative writing and measurement calculations to our daily academic log and they were able to enjoy working independently. Interestingly, each student continued to pursue his or her focus area into high school, one earning a creative writing credit and the other a personal finance credit.

As we gave our middle schoolers time to process, we saw life skills develop, time managed, and the love of learning launched. Interests were explored at a deeper level, creating independent learners, a wonderful skill to launch high school learning.

People are resources. Obviously parents are on the front line in this area; however, mentors and professionals are also an important asset. Middle schoolers learn from people in their area of interest, perhaps a store manager, dental hygienist, or war veteran. We encourage our middle and high school students to seek out people who have their strengths or who have experience in a career field of interest. As they get older, we encourage our young adults to job shadow or volunteer in as many career fields as possible. These experiences offer opportunities to gain understanding about life, but also to narrow down what careers may or may not be of consideration.

Transportation is another valuable resource. Most parents know this first hand as they become escorts to sporting events, music lessons, community service activities, and leadership opportunities for young adults who are not driving. For our family, this precious time in the car was an opportune time to process ideas, talk through difficult scenarios, role play potential interactions, and pray for whatever situations arose from the day's activities. Though the learning and service were valuable, the deepened relationships and knitted hearts were timeless. They learned what we modeled.

Middle school students are really not any different than adults. Adults thrive when they understand their strengths and have freedom to grow those strengths, when they have people to help them process ideas and thoughts, when they have access to necessary tools and resources to carry out a plan, and when they are surrounded by supportive family and friends.

A Reason to Celebrate

My son has a passion for fishing. He loves to fish, anytime, anywhere. He is observant and learns from other fishermen, hence he asks me to take him to the docks frequently. Once at the dock, he watches, curious about what test the fishermen use, what bait is working best, and if the men are using sinkers. While watching, he starts conversations, questioning how bait and line depth work together. Surprisingly, the fishermen, who usually do not share their secrets with competitors, talk to my son. They eagerly teach him their sport, fueling his interest and teaching him life and academic skills.

During his fishing adventure, my son figured out he could learn from the men at the local bait shop. He chatted with the owner to find out where fishermen were catching fish, inquired about the fish being caught, and questioned the type of bait being used. My son applied what he learned to his fishing. Interestingly as he learned he began to understand the correlation between the moon, sun and catching fish. Solunar and weather websites became his favorite reads on the Internet. He learned the major and minor windows and the moon phases. Science concepts were understood because of his passion for fishing. Finally, that winter all this hard work paid off! He caught a ten-pound large mouth bass! The fish was mounted and now graces the wall of his bedroom. He has caught many fish, including a thirty-four inch gatortrout. As part of his intrigue for fishing my son learned to clean and cook fish. His respect and love for the outdoors continued to grow.

My son wanted to take his outdoor learning one step further — making crayfish traps. He watched a plethora of how-to videos, comparing different traps and making note of materials needed for their construction. My son and I discussed his plans and purchased materials; enough to make several types of traps. Then experimentation began. He set his traps in several different freshwater creeks, checking on them several times a day. I often went with him, helping to measure the depth of the trap, another aspect of crayfish trapping my son discovered as he experimented. He caught crayfish, snakes, and turtles.

One time a trap disappeared. My son was hurt and frustrated that someone might have taken the trap. This provided a great life lesson as we processed his feelings.

My son's passion for fishing and love for the outdoors has taught him how to learn independently, to apply the scientific method, and to persevere through difficult circumstances. He has learned mistakes can be life lessons. In addition, he has gained interpersonal, mechanical, and research skills. His natural, applied learning has encompassed every subject.

One of the greatest rewards that I believe has come from our experiences together is that my son and I have shared in this learning journey and it has deepened our relationship.

I have heard the middle school years called the speed bump years; years we all have to travel through, but years that often slow us down. These years can be wasted on repeating lessons of elementary concepts or pretend warm-ups for high school studies. It is not usually a time of deep study or fostering of interests.

However, the middle school years have great potential to directly impact a student's entrepreneurial ventures, employment, or college and career path by offering options of promising study. Encouraging students to set and accomplish goals, develop personal and interpersonal skills, and build knowledge in areas of interest will greatly influence the high school years. In fact, it may also influence the college years.

As homeschool evaluators who meet with families every summer for annual evaluations, we know middle schoolers who have definite goals. Recently we met a young man who knew he wanted to be an attorney, with sights set on a highly selective university. This information is valuable to parents as well as to their eighth grader. Together they can sit down and make a plan. What classes need to be taken to make sure the student can take advanced math—calculus, analytical geometry, and trigonometry—before graduation? How can the student plan to take the three SAT II tests required by his or her top choice college? The late middle school years were vital to this motivated young man as he began completing classes he needed before he entered high school. Time management and responsibility were automatic in this student's life because he knew what he wanted to do and set out to do it well, with purpose.

Be ready for your middle schooler to surprise you! Ours have surprised us many times with their ideas and plans. They had solutions we had not discovered, insight we could not see. We had to keep our hands and minds open if we were going to walk alongside them in their journey. Often the plans or thoughts we had were vastly different than the ideas of our middle and high school students. Theirs were not only better, but because the students "owned" the plans, they were more excited and successful in executing steps to reach their goals.

Notes

Chapter 2

Navigating the Middle School Academic Maze

Middle school academics can be a maze; a turn here, a dead end there. Sometimes a path is chosen, an obstacle appears, and another path is followed. The process continues until the pencil crosses the end point and the maze is solved.

There are as many possible educational paths through middle and into high school as there are students. Why? Each student is unique in his or her strengths, interests, and goals. Consider the people you know. How did they get to where they are today? Likely, their educational and career paths were very different. Some may have learned from internships. Others may have flourished in a more academically rigorous environment. Maybe some lived overseas, learning from experience. Every journey was different. Our middle schooler's trek will be just as unique. In order to help navigate, we must understand the options in the twists and turns of the middle school maze.

Traditional Progression

What are the educational paths? Most students in public and private schools follow a traditional path, each year completing English, math, social science, science courses, and additional elective classes which might include art, computer, physical education, music, or foreign language studies. Course material is taught according to standards, often including chunks of course-specific information and subject-related vocabulary. Standards for middle school classes vary from state to state. Even with the implementation with Common Core Standards, how the standards are taught can vary greatly from classroom to classroom. There is a pre-prescribed course progression and textbooks are the primary means for learning.

- **English**

English is taken every year with studies in literature and literary form, grammar and punctuation, types of writing (narrative, expository, persuasive), the writing process (pre-writing, drafting, revising, editing, and publication), speech communication, and vocabulary development. These classes—and subsequent textbooks—are often titled English 6, English 7, and English 8. Middle school students who can read, comprehend, and complete high school level work may consider this option.

- **Math**

Math in middle school varies from a continuation and deepening investigation of foundational math skills, numbers and operations, to college preparatory Algebra I and Geometry. This progression depends on the student's mastery of concepts and aptitude for the subject. Classes are often titled Math 6, Math 7, Math 8, Pre-Algebra, Algebra I, and Geometry. Advanced high school level classes are offered to middle school students who show proficiency, likely Algebra I in seventh or eighth grade followed by Algebra II or Geometry. High school classes are planned according to which courses were completed in middle school.

- **Social Sciences**

Social sciences include American and world history, geography, world culture, and civics. Beginning in the high school years, American government, economics, psychology, and sociology are added to the repertoire of course selections.

- **Science**

Middle school science subjects can vary. Some schools offer Science 6, Science 7, and Science 8 which combine varied science topics taught at a progressively deeper level each year. Topics are selected from the areas of life science (study of living things), physical science (laws of force, motion, and speed), Earth and space science (Earth and space natural features and components), technology, the scientific method and inquiry (science-related critical thinking, communication, and analysis), and science careers. Other schools choose to offer stand alone physical science or biology courses, especially in eighth grade. These courses are often offered as a high school level option for college-bound students. Activities in science courses should include experimentation, observation, the use of related science tools, and the creation of graphs and tables to record data.

Interest-Based Learning

Home educated students have the availability of an endless selection of interest-based learning choices. Choosing an interest-based path, the student can learn consumer economics and personal finance by planning and building a business or equine science while volunteering at a horse farm. Learning can incorporate internet or community resources, primary source documents, mentorship and job shadowing opportunities, experiential activities, and interactions with professionals. Often the depth of interest-based studies can be considerably deeper than a more traditional approach to learning. Likewise, retention is generally greater as the subject of study is based on the curiosity and interest of the student. What is more, intrinsic interest has proven to produce the highest retention.

Interest-based studies tend to be integrated, much like a unit study. The learning can be multi-disciplinary incorporating study skills, research methods, written reports and essays, literature selections, vocabulary development, math computations, geography, and computer skills. Experiential activities may include building terrariums, dioramas, salt-dough maps, and interactive game boards; field trips to science centers, zoos, nature preserves, planetariums, weather stations, and museums; visits to biological and botanical parks; interactions with scientists, technical, or medical professionals; and participation in spelling bees, 4-H, scouting, history and science fairs. Interest-based learning, even if only in one or two areas of study can make a difference; in fact, it may greatly determine a student's career or college path.

Combination Approach

A combination approach weaves the traditional and interest-based models and uses the strengths of each to create a unique, custom plan for the student. The preference for math may be a traditional textbook approach covering math concepts in a progressive manner. For English, perhaps literature selections are based on a historical period corresponding with the student's choice for history study. Science may be a more traditional approach or connected with the historical period. A parent using a combination path carefully considers how the student learns best and draws curriculum and activities from everything and anything available, from books to experiences in a professional environment.

Middle school classes have the potential to build on key concepts, through deeper interactive study, foundational for understanding of high school and college level study. In the later middle school years, especially in the home study environment, high school courses can be taken if the student is ready for that level of learning and is planning on attending college.

For students who are able to handle advanced study, it is not too early to create a high school plan. College-bound middle schoolers can, and often do, take high school level courses while in seventh and eighth grade. This is especially true for Algebra I and Geometry when offered in eighth grade.

Looking Ahead to High School

Middle school is a time for looking ahead, a time for considering high school options. Some middle schoolers have definite ideas regarding what they want to study, perhaps even where they might like to attend college. For students intending to attend college, plans can be made to meet the academic requirements of the schools of choice, especially if the university is highly selective or competitive. If the student shows proficiency in a specific content area, parents must find educational options which will allow the child to excel, seeking the help of tutors or mentors if necessary.

If a student completes middle school with limited or no ideas which direction he or she may head, do not worry. Often middle school students are just catching a glimpse of what they think they may pursue. Continue to encourage strengths and interests. Offer suggestions and possibilities for making what they enjoy a springboard for learning. Think outside the box and seek experiential learning alternatives or volunteering options through which many career and professional environments can be observed. Weeding out the "no way" careers as well as narrowing down the "maybe" choices will eventually enable the young adult to hone in on the "yes!"

Wilbur and Orville Wright studied their passion deeply, reading any books they could find on the subject and seeking out experts in their field. There were no divisions in the subjects they learned or levels too high to attain. In fact, there were no grade levels assigned to their learning. They learned from their interests and were encouraged by significant people in their lives. Together the boys and their mentors, considered possibilities with no limits to how much they could learn or achieve. They reaped a great harvest from the efforts, the achievement of their goal as well as the ability to change history. Could your middle schooler forge the next greatest impact on the community, nation, and the world? Indeed, I think so! That's a great reason to begin celebrating high school in middle school.

Chapter 3

Middle School Record Keeping

Every year families come to our kitchen table to share their accomplishments, work samples and activity logs in hand. Our time together is celebratory, a time of reflection as well as a time of looking forward. Though recordkeeping takes time to sustain, the results are valuable, testifying to where we have been and guiding our next steps.

Keeping a Middle School Portfolio

The purpose of any portfolio of work samples is to verify course content and record the progress of the student. Portfolios are required by some state statutes. In our state, there is no statutory difference between an elementary collection of work and a middle school compilation.

Work samples vary from course to course. Math samples might include problems from the lessons, scratch work, and tests. Research papers, writing assignments, book summaries, vocabulary lists, and a literature list give insight into language arts progress. Social sciences and science work samples will vary dependent on the teaching method used. As home education evaluators, my husband and I have seen arrays of map work, timelines, interviews, lab reports, photos of dissections, as well as summaries of shadowing experiences and brochures from experiential learning opportunities. Digital portfolios are increasingly popular as young adults learn to use software applications. If the student is a budding graphic artist or photographer, this venue may be especially appealing. Young entrepreneurs can include examples of their media packets, promotional materials, or visual presentations of business opportunities. Musicians may consider digital recordings of their work. If the student plans to attend art school, starting an art portfolio may be fitting.

A motivated middle school student is able to earn credit for high school level material. Saving work samples may be wise should the student have to verify completion. As the student enters high school, consider compiling a cumulative folder of high school records where supporting documents needed for employment or college admission can be saved. The section about cumulative high school records on page 96 might be helpful.

Creating a Middle School Report Card

No need for panic! Report cards are rarely needed. In my twenty-two years of home education I have had to create only three, two for students in our family and one for a student of a friend. So, why include rarely needed information in this book? Because I wish I would have had resources at my fingertips when I was required to produce a middle school report card for an intramural sports team—with no advanced notice. I wondered what to include on the document and how to best format the information. Research took a few hours. If including what I learned helps another parent celebrate the middle school years, it is worth the ink.

Report cards offer a snapshot of academic achievement for a designated period of time, generally on the quarter schedule, every nine weeks. Traditional report cards denote one grade for each subject. Though there is a growing trend toward standard-based report cards—a result of standard-driven education—I chose a traditional format. I felt it would best represent the education of our middle schooler. Report cards are most likely needed when applying for special courses outside the home, competing in local sports organizations, or submitting scholarship applications.

Though homeschool families in most states are not bound to this type of documentation or or grade schedule, it is helpful to have some background knowledge should your middle schooler need to comply with this requirement.

Record Keeping Tip

Writing a Middle School Report Card

There were occasions when we needed to create a middle school report card, for example when our entrepreneur was applying for a young business owner's scholarship or when our bowler wanted to join the local league. Like many homeschooling moms, the first request caught me surprised, blindsided.

I started researching and talking to other moms who had walked the report card journey. There are common elements, some situation specific, on report cards.

- Student name
- Parent/guardian name(s)
- Home address
- Contact information
- Date of issue
- Quarterly grades
- Final grades
- Comments on behavior
- Grading scale (percentage or adjective)
- Official parent/guardian signature

Public and privates schools designate space to comment on the student's work effort and personal development. Creating my middle school report cards, I decided these components were outside the scope of what the entities requested.

Official Report
Card
Jeffery D. Jones
April 3, 2016

Student Name Jeffery D. Jones
Date of Birth: December 21, 2002
Address: 123 Spencer Road
Circle City, NE 00000

School: Homeschool
Parents: Timothy and Susan Jones
Phone: 123-456-7890
Email: middleschoolstudent@everylink.com

Academic Year : 2015-2016 (Grade 7)					
Subject	1st Quarter	2nd Quarter	3rd Quarter	4th Quarter	Final Grade
English Language Arts	A	A	B		
Pre-Algebra	A	B	A		
Earth Science	A	A	A		
European History	A	A	A		
Health and Nutrition	A	A	A		
Introduction to Aviation	A	A	A		
Sculpture	A	A	A		

Explanation of Grades
A Excellent
B Above Average
C Average
D Difficulty
F Failing

_____
Joseph W. Jones, Parent

_____
Contact Phone Number

_____
Date

Official Report Card
Jeffery D. Jones
Academic Year 2015-2016

Student Name: Jeffery D. Jones
Date of Birth: December 21, 2002
Address: 123 Spencer Road
    Circle City, NE 00000

School: Homeschool
Parents: Timothy and Susan Jones
Phone: 123-456-7890
Email: middleschoolstudent@everylink.com

Date of Issue: October 2, 2015

Student Academic Record

Academic Year: 2014-2015 (Grade 6)

Subject	First Quarter	Second Quarter	Thrid Quarter	Fourth Quarter	Final Grade
English Language Arts	A	A	A	A	A
Math 6	A	B	A	A	A
Life Science	A	A	A	A	A
American History	A	A	A	A	A
Introductory Spanish	A	A			A
Small Engine Repair	A	A			A
Woodworking			A	A	A
Drawing and Painting			A	A	A

Academic Year: 2015-2016 (Grade 7)

Subject	First Quarter	Second Quarter	Thrid Quarter	Fourth Quarter	Final Grade
English Language Arts	A				
Pre-Algebra	B				
Earth Science	A				
European History	A				
Health and Nutrition	A				
Introduction to Aviation	A				
Sculpture	A				

Grading Scale: 90-100 A   80-89 B   70-79 C

Timothy W. Jones, Parent

Contact Phone Number

Date

Chapter 4

Future Possibilities

Possibilities abound! Just as each middle and high school student is unique in talents, interests, and strengths, so are the possibilities before and after graduation. The potential choices for a student's next steps may be evident and obvious, or they may not. There could be opportunities for job shadowing, mentorships, travel experiences, volunteer work, leadership roles, sports participation, or employment. As these experiential learning options present themselves, parents should look for hints of willingness and motivation in their student and be ready to help him or her process thoughts and ideas. By keeping an open mind, parents give their student the best chance of being ready for the possibilities which come his or her way.

Ponder the Potential of Experiential Learning

Experiential learning does not have to end in elementary school. Often as parents see middle school and high school resting on the not-too-distant horizon, there is a temptation to "buckle down", in other words, start checking boxes so the child will be ready for high school and beyond. In the wake remains the student's strengths, interests, and learning style, the very things which could propel the student toward a career choice. While care must be taken to meet college admission requirements, there must also be care taken to preserve the interests and heart of the young adult. A well-educated bitter person is not what parents hope to have at the end of their educational journey together.

I understand the choices, the boxes, the entire scenario. I walked this road with my oldest the first year of high school. Knowing he would go to college, likely a competitive one, we planned out his four-year path. It was packed with academics, the classes he needed. I planned right over the electives and left no white space. I could not think outside the box; in fact, the only thing I saw was entrance to college. He would have met the requirements but "looked" like everyone else on paper--nothing unique or intriguing.

Thankfully, my mind and eyes were opened. I saw the benefit of real-life experiences and conversations with professionals in high school. I learned I did not have to give up this wonderful means of learning in the later years of education. I also realized the great impact of job shadowing, mentoring, travel, and community involvement, just in time for sophomore year planning.

We purposed to make our son's next year different by adding course content and experiences he felt would be helpful. One of his great strengths was reading. He loved to read, especially in the areas of history and business. I compiled the literature lists on page 102 to give him some direction and then allowed him the freedom to choose literature and independent reading selections. He recorded title and author on a computer document. In the end, he chose better pieces of literature than I could have imagined!

I also pondered how I could add experiential learning to every high school course. I found this a bit difficult for math. I thought about people we knew, people our son could job shadow, places we could visit, venues where he could serve—all while learning. As I thought, I considered how I could maximize the potential of experiential learning opportunities for my son. In doing so I had to be knowledgeable about my son, his interests, and his goals. I also had to have a willingness to think outside the box. I had to observe strengths, encourage answers, team up with resources, and enlist mentors.

- **Observe Strengths**

Often strengths manifest early in children, before middle school. The child might have a knack for encouraging others (consider volunteering at a nursing home or preschool) or planning events (consider planning a birthday party for younger sibling). Maybe he or she sees the world spatially (consider job shadowing an interior designer) or has an eye for color (consider job shadowing an graphic artist or assisting a photographer). Parents play a vital role in identifying strengths, verbalizing what those strengths are, and then encouraging the development of those strengths. Just as adults often do not understand their strengths, children do not either unless we as parents affirm them and encourage their use. These strengths may lead to securing employment, choosing a college, or selecting a career choice.

- **Encourage Interests**

Interests often fuel a desire to learn more. Think about your interests. You want to learn more about those interests, right? So do our children. Interests make great springboards for observation hours, travel, and community involvement or service. Middle and high schoolers need us to affirm their interests, to walk alongside them as they build on their interests, and to provide encouragement as they pursue their interests. For instance, a young adult interested in personal finance may benefit from conversations with financial planners. A budding guitarist might enjoy being on the worship team at church, playing at a local venue, or composing his or her own music and lyrics. Student artists and writers could earn scholarship monies from contests and art displays. There are as many options for learning experiences as there are interests. Hence, it takes the creative thinking of the parent and student to brainstorm possibilities.

- **Team Up with Resources**

Middle and high school students need resources to learn. Resources may include informational references, tools and materials, mentors, venues, and time. If the cost of any resource exceeds the family budget, consider bartering. To illustrate, a horse enthusiast may volunteer at a barn in exchange for lessons, an artist may choose to volunteer at an event in exchange for a display space, or a young adult could offer babysitting in exchange for music lessons. In reality, a course might need to be postponed to make room in the day for experiential opportunities. With endless possibilities, time needs to be set aside for brainstorming and processing.

- **Enlist Mentors**

As a parent, I value mentors who teach skills and concepts, often experientially. Mentors have played a significant role in the lives of our middle and high school as instruction occurred on-site or on the job, demonstrating know-how that books could not teach. As a young adult expressed an interest, we began to pray and consider who might be a good role model, an experienced tradesperson, or professional influence. Mentoring experiences can be some of the most beneficial learning opportunities in the lives of our middle and high schoolers.

Building on the strengths of my at-home students, using interests to enhance learning, looking for and finding resources, and enlisting the help of mentors greatly impacted the depth and meaning of our high schoolers' educational paths. Perhaps more importantly, our future young adults were offered life-changing community service opportunities and significant additions to their college applications.

A Reason to Celebrate

The elementary years were non-stop action for our second son, a kinesthetic learner. Middle school was full of outdoor learning and scouting adventures. Reading and writing were not priorities or strengths for this son. Interpersonal skills were another story! He loved people, caring deeply about how they felt and what they needed. He was a help and an encouragement to anyone, regardless of age.

Enter the high school years. School work was completed, but scouting and sports were the highlights of his days. He completed his Eagle Scout project and mentored younger scouts in outdoor living, first aid, and survival skills. Earning his Eagle Scout rank was a tremendous accomplishment and honor.

We remained faithful to meet typical high school requirements — even though it took extra time and patience to complete the work — to give this student a foundational working vocabulary in the core content areas. Together, we discussed future possibilities with our son, keeping all options open, not knowing whether he would seek employment or college admission after high school.

During his senior year we considered dual enrollment at the state college. This experience would give him a chance to understand the expectations of college courses in a smaller setting than a large university lecture hall. Our son prepared for and took the college placement exam, scoring high enough to take College Algebra. We were thrilled, me especially because I did not have to teach Algebra II. We asked other homeschooling parents for professor recommendations and checked Rate My Professors online.

The course was tremendous. The professor made himself available to the students. We helped our son understand how he learned best, and encouraged him to seek out like-minded students for study sessions. The experience gave him confidence. He finished the semester with an "A."

After high school graduation, our son enrolled full time in the state college, completing his Associate in Arts degree. An elective course helped him discover how much he enjoyed rehabilitation services, finally choosing physical therapy after shadowing and working at a local clinic. School, once a task to finish, something to be done, was now embraced because of his desire to learn more about his chosen field. The confidence gained from dual enrollment helped him realize he could succeed at college work. He maintained a 4.0 GPA through his Associate in Arts degree program, which provided a scholarship toward his Bachelor of Science degree. Today he is preparing for the GRE and submitting applications to graduate schools to earn the required Doctor of Physical Therapy degree needed to be a licensed physical therapist. Time, maturation, experience, and interest came together.

Employment Sets a Stage

High school students often seek employment before graduation. Employment offers a means to learn more about one's self as well as potential career fields. Employment also provides a venue to develop and apply life skills, including time management, self-discipline, and work ethic—all needed for post secondary education as well as for life.

Employment offers young adults an opportunity to learn important information about how, where, when and with whom they work best. Helpful questions to process include the following:

- During which part of the day do you work best?
- Do you work better indoors or outdoors?
- Is there a skill or task you enjoy most?
- Is there a skill or task you do not enjoy?
- Do I prefer working with people or working alone?

Obtaining a job in an area of interest offers an chance to experience the many facets of a career, first-hand. High school students also catch a glimpse of options within a career field. For example, a student working in a rehabilitation clinic can observe physical therapists, occupational therapists, athletic trainers, and message therapists. Each professional works to rehabilitate patients—some pediatrics and others geriatrics, some athletes and others stroke patients—but in varied modalities. Learning the options in a specific field allows the student to fine tune employment or educational paths before taking his or her first steps after graduation, ultimately saving time and money for unnecessary college courses.

Imagine a ninth grade female student with an eye for color, line, and shape—elements of photography. Over six months time, the young adult researches camera features and costs. She continues to develop her photography skills, using online tutorials, library resources, and professional journals. Money earned babysitting is saved toward the purchase of a camera. Meanwhile, a neighbor, seeing the young lady photographing flowers in the front year, offers her the use of his camera for a few weeks. A month later the neighbor mentions he is considering selling the camera and inquires whether the student is interested in purchasing. Using her savings, she buys the camera and enrolls in an online photography class, bettering her skills. Her mother awards her one high school credit for the research, photography, and online class.

Motivated by the class, the student expresses an interest in a photography career with no intention of attending college. She is encouraged to job shadow a self-employed photographer, a family friend. The student accompanies the woman to weddings, assisting where she is able. The photographer and the student talk between shoots, discussing the photographer's education and experience. At the photographer's suggestion, the student decides to take Spanish in her sophomore year so she can communicate with future clients. Later in the school year, the student inquires about working at a local camera shop to gain a different perspective of the photography industry.

By the end of her junior year, the student shadows a self-employed wedding photographer, studies features of current camera models on the market, improves communication skills with co-workers and customers, and learns aspects of running a photography business. Managing her time well is a necessity in order to complete her high school courses. One of the personal contacts at the shop tells the student about a job as an assistant to a local photographer who specializes in family portraiture. She applies, then finishes her senior year and graduates from home, continuing to work part-time at the camera shop while starting her own photography business.

The student's interest in photography contributed to her learning time management, self-discipline, work ethics, and interpersonal communication skills. Employment, especially in a field of interest, can solidify a strength, influence high school courses options, or confirm a career choice—a worthwhile endeavor, indeed.

A Reason to Celebrate

The inspiration for my career came during my first year of homeschooling. I was six years old and met a neighbor girl. She was Deaf and used American Sign Language. I could not communicate with her. I was devastated. My amazing mother—knowing the ache I felt to befriend our neighbor—had the flexibility and insight to pile my sisters and brother in the van for an impromptu library trip. We searched the library shelves for sign language books appropriate for a first grader. We borrowed a Sesame Street sign language phrase book. Eventually, after checking out the book many, many times, my parents bought me a personal copy. I still own that book today.

Over the years my parents and I prayed God would bring sign language resources into my life. One time our van broke down in the middle of nowhere and in the closest house resided a teenage boy who was Deaf. My Dad came back to employ my meager assistance in communicating with the young man. Thrilled with my enthusiasm and effort, he gave me an ASL dictionary. My knowledge of vocabulary soared, but my understanding of syntax was weak.

When I was in middle school, our church hired a new senior pastor. Amazingly, not only was his wife a homeschooling mom but she was also a sign language interpreter. She agreed to teach me and my friends after church on Sundays. I began to put signs together in the appropriate order and continued to meet people in the Deaf culture. I read every single book in the Orange County Library on deafness, the Deaf culture, and American Sign Language. Around the same time, we moved to Seminole County. Their system offered many new titles pertinent to my study.

When I was a junior in high school we called the closest elementary school to our house. It "happened" to be the only hub for elementary Deaf education in our county. As part of my research to learn if Deaf education was the path I wanted to pursue in college, we inquired as to whether I could volunteer during summer school. They welcomed me with open arms. Little did we know this would be the school at which I would begin my career after graduating from college—and remain for my first nine years—as an educational interpreter for the Deaf.

Today, as a homeschooling mom, I continue to pursue my passion by occasionally freelancing as an interpreter for the Deaf in my community; interpreting at church, teaching ASL classes to homeschooled students, and teaching my own children how to sign from infancy. What a blessing to have had parents who gave me the flexibility and freedom of an education which allowed me to pursue an interest which became a passion, a career, and a ministry, enriching my life and the lives of others.

Chapter 5

Plan Well to Finish Well

Celebrations take planning. High school is no exception. Considering employment options, building a resume, touring college campuses, preparing for testing, and submitting application are just some of the possible junctions in the high school journey. Planning in advance for these significant mile markers is essential to finishing the high school journey with excellence.

Develop a Four-Year Plan

Most middle school parents begin to develop a flexible (yes, in pencil) high school academic plan as early as seventh and eighth grade so their students can consider taking high school level classes in late middle school. This is especially helpful for students who excel in math or who have a linguistic gifting and want to begin work in foreign languages.

Beginning the second semester of eighth grade, parents begin to think even more seriously about high school. To do so, they begin researching statute mandates, career choices, merit scholarships, graduation requirements, college admission, and collegiate sports involvement, all of which are expounded upon in this book. Brainstorming course options with these aspects in mind, while being attentive to the student's learning style and strengths, will help devise a plan with the greatest possibilities for success. The discussions resulting from brainstorming potential make for beneficial conversations, helping to keep hearts and minds open and growing relationships.

Parents often feel they must voice their opinions and thoughts as students makes course and career choices. This is usually done with the good intentions of hoping students will have the best possible outcomes. After all, if the young adult does well in high school, is admitted to a well-known college, and graduates with honors, life will be good, right? Sometimes, but not always. Life is not predictable and there are no easy solutions. In the process of trying to "make it all happen" the parent-child relationship often becomes strained.

While helping my first high school student navigate important planning decisions, I found it difficult to balance my well-intentioned plans with his thoughts and aspirations. He had definite goals and ideas about how to obtain his ambitions. Yes, I could offer constructive input based on experience and aged-wisdom, but ultimately the plan could not be my plan. After all, I was not the one who was going to live out the details or the results. When I discovered a balance between telling and listening, the relationship with my son became stronger and I was invited into conversation. In other words, my opinion was sought after and my son was more willing to listen. The four-year plan was valuable, but not as important as the relationship with my son.

Record Keeping Tip

Develop a Four-Year Plan

Before developing a four-year plan, these are important details to gather:
- Any state statutory requirements for home educated students
- State high school graduation requirements if required for home educated students
- Career goals
- Course pre-requisites or skills needed for future employment
- Course requirements for state merit scholarship application and eligibility
- Courses and content which may be helpful for SAT, ACT, or college admission testing preparation
- College admission requirements for top colleges of choice
- NCAA requirements for student athletes pursuing collegiate sports

A Reason to Celebrate

When we went on vacation we visited colleges along the way. If we traveled to a sports event, we visited a college. We quickly learned our young adult preferred a small campus where professors could provide personal attention to students. This information narrowed is his top college choices, hence research time.

Our next step was to research and compare admission requirements for his top colleges, a few highly selective. From our comparison, we were able to adjust our original four-year plan to account for the courses needed: four English credits (English I with American Literature, English II with World Literature, English III with British Literature, and English IV with Contemporary Literature); three math credits (Algebra I, Geometry, and Algebra II); three social science credits (American History, World History, American Government, and Economics); and three science credits (Biology, Chemistry, and Physics). Two of the colleges required an additional math credit. We tentatively added the possibility of dual enrollment to our four-year plan to pick up college algebra. Foreign language was required by two universities. We added those two credits to our planning worksheet. With all potential course requirements accounted for, and several electives of interest, the revision of our four-year plan was complete.

Planning Ahead

9th Grade	10th Grade	11th Grade	12th Grade
• Research course requirements for employment or career choice.	• Evaluate long-term goals and update the four-year plan.	• Evaluate long-term goals and four-year plan. Discuss options after graduation.	• Evaluate long-term goals and four-year plan. Consider internships.
• Research admission requirements for colleges of choice as well as state, merit, and college scholarships.	• Register for PSAT in early August for the October test date.	• Consider online, dual enrollment, AP classes, and CLEP testing.	• Consider online classes, dual enrollment, AP classes and CLEP testing.
• Make a tentative four-year course plan.	• Visit www.collegeboard.com. Plan to take the SAT and ACT. Note registration deadlines.	• Register for PSAT in early August for the October test date.	• Visit www.collegeboard.com. Plan to take the SAT and ACT. Note registration deadlines.
• Begin preparation for the PSAT.	• Research SAT Subject Tests. Determine which, if any, are needed for college admission. These are generally needed by selective colleges.	• Visit www.collegeboard.com. Detail a plan for taking the SAT and ACT. Note registration deadlines.	• Review college admission deadlines.
• Visit and tour college campuses.	• Prepare for the SAT and ACT.	• Visit and tour college campuses. Attend local college fairs.	• Write essays. Finalize transcript format and content. Submit final transcript after graduation.
• Begin community service, logging hours, obtaining verification on company letterhead.	• Research state merit scholarship requirements. Plan how requirements will be met and go beyond the minimum requirements in case changes are made. *Florida residents: Check Bright Futures website for most current requirements.*	• Contact the state scholarship office. Recheck requirements and ask questions regarding student records. Keep a log of your questions and answers for future reference.	• Apply to colleges of choice by October. Research proves students who apply early (not necessarily early decision) receive better scholarship opportunities.
• Write course descriptions for current classes, begin a reading list, and draft a transcript format.	• Research NCAA scholarship requirements and guidelines for home educated students.	• Research NCAA scholarship requirements for home educated students. Meet with current and college coaches.	• File taxes and submit the Free Application for Federal Student Aid (FAFSA) after January 1 but before March 1.
	• Keep course descriptions, reading lists, and transcript current.	• Keep course descriptions, reading lists, and transcript current.	• Complete and submit paperwork for state merit scholarships. (*Bright Futures*)
	• Visit and tour college campuses. Attend local college fairs.	• Check out new student information online and become familiar with applications from colleges of choice.	• Reply to college acceptance letters and financial aid offers. Notify colleges if you decline offers.
		• Check financial aid information. Research private financial aid resources and local scholarship opportunities.	• Fill out remaining admission paperwork. Submit payments. Verify immunizations.
		• List admission deadlines for colleges of choice.	• Submit final transcript after graduation.
		• Practice interviews.	

This table created for inclusion in *Celebrate High School,* fourth edition © 2015 by Cheryl Bastian. For more information about this publication, please contact the author or visit her website at www.cherylbastian.com.

General Graduation Guidelines for Colleges and Universities

Graduation requirements vary from state to state, university to university, hence the variable credit guidelines detailed below. Research your state's graduation requirements as well as college admission requirements for colleges of interest. Aim above the minimum. This chart guides parents who desire to build a competitive student profile, for entrance to the workforce or the university. These guidelines should not be taken as educational or legal counsel.

Content Area	General High School Graduation	College Preparatory (College-bound)	College Preparatory (High Selective College)
English	4 credits	4 credits	4 or more credits
Math	3 credits	4 credits *generally Algebra I and above	4 or more credits *may depend on intended major
Social Studies	3 credits	3 or 4 credits	4 or more credits *may depend on intended major
Science	3 credits	3 or 4 credits *2 or 3 with lab	4 or more credits *may depend on intended major
Foreign Language	2 credits *may not be required	2 credits	3 or 4 credits
Performing /Fine Arts	1 credit	1 or 2 credits	1 or 2 credits
Physical Education	1 credit	1 credits	1 or 2 credits
Electives	5 to 8 credits *may include trade or vocational skills for students considering trade careers	6 to 8 credits *consider academic electives for college preparatory	6 to 8 credits *students applying to highly selective schools should consider additional academic electives in their intended major
Total	**20 to 24 credits**	**24 to 28 credits**	**26 to 30 credits**

Four-Year Plan for High School Students - Worksheet

Student_____ Date _____ Anticipated Graduation Date_____

Core Courses	8th Grade (High School Level)	9th Grade	10th Grade	11th Grade	12th Grade
English *Includes literature, vocabulary and substantial composition.*					
Math *Generally includes Algebra I, Algebra II, and Geometry*					
Social Studies *Generally includes American History, World History, American Government and Economics*					
Natural Sciences *Generally includes Biology, Chemistry and Physics (often two must include lab)*					
Foreign Language *Generally two CONSECUTIVE years of same language*					
Performing/ Fine Arts					
Business/ Computer Technology					
Physical Education					
Electives *May include academic electives*					

- Refer to page 40 for general graduation guidelines. Consider student's interests when planning.
- Refer to page 43 for specific Bright Futures requirements.
- **General Guideline:** Six credits per year, working four to six hours a day. Many home educated students earn more than six credits per year, especially if they earn credits over the summer. More credits may be needed to meet the requirements for admission to highly-selective, competitive universities.

Sample Four-Year High School Plan for Students
*These classes are selected as a sample ONLY.

Student: *Annie Smith*   **Date:** *August 24, 2015*   **Anticipated Graduation Date:** *May 24, 2019*

Core Courses	8th Grade (High School Level)	9th Grade	10th Grade	11th Grade	12th Grade
English		English I: Survey of American Literature (1)	English II: Survey of World Literature (1)	English III: Survey of Ancient World Literature (1)	English IV: Survey of Contemporary Literature (1)
Math	Algebra I (1)	Geometry (1)	Algebra II (1)	Trigonometry/ Analytical Geometry (1)	Calculus (academic elective) (1)
Social Studies		American History (1)	Modern World History (1)	Ancient World History (1)	American Government (0.5) Economics (0.5)
Natural Sciences		Biology (with lab) (1)	Chemistry (with lab) (1)	Physics (with lab) (1)	Human Anatomy and Physiology (academic elective) (1)
Foreign Language				Spanish I (1)	Spanish II (1)
Performing/ Fine Arts		Drawing and Painting I (1)			
Physical Education		Personal Fitness (0.5)		Nutrition and Wellness (0.5)	
Electives		Drama I (1)	Speech I (1) Driver's Education (0.5) Web Design (0.5)	Speech II (1) Shakespearean Literature and Theater (0.5)	Photography I (1)

Total Credits 26.5

- Refer to page 40 for general graduation guidelines. Use State Department of Education graduation requirements as reference.
- Refer to page 43 for specific Bright Futures requirements.
- Outside Florida, be sure to check statutory requirements in regards to home education and state graduation requirements, as well as state merit scholarships available to home educators.

FL

Public School Graduation Requirements

Graduation requirements vary from state to state. If you are high schooling in a state other than Florida, research your state graduation requirements as determined by the state Department of Education. Inquire whether those requirements are compulsory for home educated students. Once this information is known, parents can develop a four-year high school plan.

State graduation requirements can be used as a guideline when developing the four-year plan for a homeschooled high schooler. There are several reasons why using the graduation requirements as a guideline is wise. First, home educated students compete with public and private school students for college admission. Though homeschooled students often excel academically when compared to peers, there have been situations where families have not considered state graduation requirements and later been disappointed when their young adult was not accepted for college admission. Second, some parents use the graduation requirements as a guideline incase unforeseen circumstances require the student to be enrolled in a local public or private school at some point in the high school journey. Finally, some parents, anxious they lack the knowledge needed to home educate through high school, consider the graduation requirements helpful. These are all legitimate concerns parents face. On the other hand, there are parents who never consider graduation requirements and develop a distinctive course plan based on the interests and giftings of the student. Ultimately, every family's high school journey will differ based upon their educational philosophy, the student's career goals, and the educational opportunities and options available.

Public School Graduation Requirements for the State of Florida

According to the Florida Statues, at the printing of this book, there are **no** specific graduation requirements for home educated students. However, it is wise to understand what the state requires in the event the student is no longer enrolled as a home educated student. Laws and requirements change; it is the parent's responsibility to research the most current graduation requirements and ask questions of knowledgeable personnel. Refer to the Florida Department of Education website for the most up-to-date information.

Florida Bright Futures Scholarship

Florida home education students who meet the home education criteria for Bright Futures Scholarship are eligible for either the Academic Scholars or the Medallion Scholars level. At the time of this publication, the Gold Seal Vocational Scholars award was not available to home educated students.

From our experience, and the experiences of other home education families we know, it is important to consider crucial aspects of the scholarship.

- **Plan ahead!** Often families research Bright Futures requirements too late in the high school journey and miss significant eligibility requirements. The students became ineligible for scholarship funds because of lack of planning.

- Check for changes to any aspects of Bright Futures including eligibility, funds disbursement, duration of awards, and reinstatement. **Keep current!**

- Apply for the scholarship even if the student accepts out of state admission, takes a gap year between high school and college, attends a military academy, or does not plan on attending college. We know students in these situations. When plans changed a year or two later, the students were ineligible because they did not apply at the time of graduation.

- **Be familiar eligibility requirements.** These differ for public, private, and home educated students. If the student was enrolled in a public or private school prior to enrolling in the county home education program, read the document prepared for home educated students.

  ⌨ http://www.floridastudentfinancialaid.org/SSFAD/bf/pdf/BFHomeEdManual.pdf

- The student must be registered in the home education program in eleventh and twelfth grades.

- Serve and document community service hours during the high school years, before graduation.

- Take the designated tests prior to June 30 of the senior year and send to at least one Florida university, state college, or public high school.

- Award amounts differ. Detailed information for award amounts, duration of award, renewal information, and summer funding are available on the Bright Futures website.

  ⌨ http://www.floridastudentfinancialaid.org/SSFAD/bf/bfmain.htm

What about Parent-Generated Transcripts?

"Bright Futures does not accept parent-generated home-education transcripts." This is one of the most misunderstood statements in the Bright Futures requirements. The parent-generated transcript is not accepted because according to Florida law, statute 1002.01 the home education program is a "sequentially progressive instruction of a student directed by his or her parent." Because the parent is directing the education, Bright Futures cannot request, accept, or determine the validity of the transcript.

At the time of printing, only requisite test scores and documentation of community services hours are required for students enrolled in the home education program according to s. 1002.41. The student must be enrolled in home education for both 11th and 12th grades. Parents should keep current on legislative changes to ensure eligibility requirements have not changed, as it is their responsibility to direct the education of their students. Seek legal counsel should there be questions.

Eligibility for Bright Futures Scholarships (May 2015) - Confirm beyond this date

	Florida Academic Scholars Award	Florida Medallion Scholars Award
Home Educated Students Students enrolled in county home education program	Students enrolled in a home education program according to s. 1002.41 during the 11th and 12th grade, with a 1290 SAT composite score or 29 ACT. GPA is not used.	Students enrolled in a home education program according to s. 1002.41 during the 11th and 12th grade, with a 1220 SAT composite score or 27 ACT **OR** 1170 SAT or 26 ACT with weighted GPA in 16 required credits below documented through public, DOE registered private school, FLVS, or dual enrollment transcripts.
Award Level Amounts www.floridastudentfinancialaid.org/SSFAD/PDF/BFHandbookChapter2.pdf#page=5	***Public Institution*** Students receive a specified, cost per credit hour, award as determined by the Florida Legislature. Award amounts are available the summer after legislative session.	***Public Institution*** Students receive a specified, cost per credit hour, award as determined by the Florida Legislature. Award amounts are available the summer after legislative session.
	Private Institution Students receive a specified, cost per credit hour, award as determined by the Florida Legislature. Award amounts are available the summer after legislative session.	***Private Institution*** Students receive a specified, cost per credit hour, award as determined by the Florida Legislature. Award amounts are available the summer after legislative session.
Grade Point Average (weighting for more challenging courses is .50 per course per year) *GPA's are not rounded	3.5 weighted GPA using the credits listed below, combined with the test scores and community service hours listed below.	3.0 weighted GPA using the credits listed below, combined with the test scores and community service hours listed below.
Required Credits	Courses must include 16 credits of college preparatory academic courses. **4 English** (3 with substantial writing) **4 Mathematics** (Algebra I and above) **3 Natural Science** (2 with substantial lab) **3 Social Science** **2 Foreign Language** (in the same language) **Total 16 credits** May use up to 2 additional credits from courses in academic areas listed above and/or AP, IB, or AICE fine arts courses to raise the GPA.	Courses must include 16 credits of college preparatory academic courses. **4 English** (3 with substantial writing) **4 Mathematics** (Algebra I and above) **3 Natural Science** (2 with substantial lab) **3 Social Science** **2 Foreign Language** (in the same l language) **Total 16 credits** May use up to 2 additional credits from courses in academic areas listed above and/or AP, IB, or AICE fine arts courses to raise the GPA.
Community Service	100 hours as approved by the DOE, district or private school	75 hours as approved by the DOE, district or private school
Test Scores Sections of the SAT, ACT and PERT from different test dates may be used to meet test criteria. For spring eligibility, test dates through January 31 are accepted. For summer eligibility, test dates through June 30 are accepted.	Best composite score of 1290 SAT (Reading and Math only) or 29 ACT (excluding writing) • Writing sections for both the SAT and ACT are not used in the composite score. • SAT Subject Tests are not used for Bright Futures eligibility. • ACT scores are rounded up for scores with 0.5 and higher, SAT scores are not rounded.	Best composite score of 1170 SAT (Reading and Math only) or 26 ACT (excluding writing) • Writing sections for both the SAT and ACT are not used in the composite score. • SAT Subject Tests are not used for Bright Futures eligibility. • ACT scores are rounded up for scores with 0.5 and higher, SAT scores are not rounded.

Parents have the sole responsibility for their child's education. This chart is intended as a guideline.
Requirements subject to change with each legislative session.
Visit the Bright Futures office or visit website for details.
🖳 http://www.floridastudentfinancialaid.org/SSFAD/PDF/BFHandbookChapter1.pdf

Test Score Requirements for Florida Bright Futures Scholarship
(2014-2015 and 2015-2016)

FL

Graduation Year	Public and Private School Students	Home Educated Students
2014-2015	**Florida Academic Scholars** SAT 1290 ACT 29 **Florida Medallion Scholars** SAT 1170 ACT 26	**Florida Academic Scholars** SAT 1290 ACT 29 **Florida Medallion Scholars** SAT 1220 ACT 27
2015-2016	**Florida Academic Scholars** SAT 1290 ACT 29 **Florida Medallion Scholars** SAT 1170 ACT 26	**Florida Academic Scholars** SAT 1290 ACT 29 **Florida Medallion Scholars** SAT 1220 ACT 27

Important Bright Futures Resources

Main Page

🖳 http://www.floridastudentfinancialaid.org/SSFAD/bf/bfmain.htm

Home Education Student Guide

🖳 http://www.floridastudentfinancialaid.org/SSFAD/bf/pdf/BFHomeEdManual.pdf

Legislative Updates

🖳 http://www.floridastudentfinancialaid.org/SSFAD/home/latestInfo.pdf

Award Amounts

🖳 http://www.floridastudentfinancialaid.org/SSFAD/PDF/BFHandbookChapter2.pdf#page=5

Bright Futures Eligibility and Award Chart (by high school graduation year)

🖳 http://www.floridastudentfinancialaid.org/SSFAD/PDF/BFEligibilityAwardChart.pdf

Chapter 6

Meeting College Admission Requirements

College admission requirements vary greatly. Some colleges require SAT or ACT test results. Others require a fine arts portfolio or perhaps an interview with college officials. A growing number of colleges are now providing test optional alternatives. Because of this variance, knowing what colleges request or require of applicants is the first step in planning well for a young adult's postsecondary future.

You may have started reading this page and thought,
We do not need this. Our young adult is not college bound or even remotely interested in college.

I encourage you to read on. There are a plethora of possibilities set out on the horizon of the next four years—maybe five or six if you are planning in middle school. Families have made similar statements only to find their young adult on a very different path than expected. Great changes often take place during the junior and senior years. Keep hands and doors open so the student is not short-changed in the last years. Anything is possible. Minds and hearts change.

The BIG Comparison

Home educated students intending to go to college—and even those who are remotely considering it—will benefit from anticipating admission requirements. This is helpful no matter where the student plans to attend: private or public, non-competitive or highly selective. Knowing what will be required will not only help parents and students to know what paperwork and testing will be needed but also whether the student has the maturity and personal readiness for college life and academics.

More and more colleges and universities offer an admissions page specifically for homeschooled applicants. I always look for this page. Another helpful page is the profiles of admitted students. This page contains data and figures for the most recently admitted class and can be helpful when determining whether the college or university may be a good fit for a student. Average test scores, class rank, GPAs, selected majors, and cultural demographics are just a few of the categories found on the page. Though this resource can be a helpful guideline, I did not allow the statistics to limit application to the college, especially in the case of test scores. A student may not have high test scores but may excel in other areas the school is seeking. Use the valuable information and disregard the rest.

As the young adult enters and moves through high school, parents—us included—have found it helpful to make a "top five" or "top ten" list of colleges the student may consider attending. This list can be kept on a spreadsheet application where specifics and special notes can be placed in columns and compared. Recording maximum admission requirements across the field of college choices reduces the chances that a student will fail to meet any college application deadlines. The spreadsheet can be updated as requirements change or as the student adds or deletes colleges from the list of top choices.

Record Keeping Tip
The BIG Comparison

A "top five" or "top ten" list can be helpful when comparing college admission requirements and deadlines. This list is easily maintained on a spreadsheet application. When compiling your student's list consider column headings most pertinent to his or her needs and interests.

- Name of college
- Location
- Size and enrollment
- Tuition costs
- Room and board costs
- Majors of interest offered
- Minors or interest offered
- Application fee
- Application deadline
- Website URL
- Courses required for admission
- Application requirements (Note whether college specific or Common Application is accepted.)
- Supplemental requirements (Forms, essays, course descriptions, reading lists, and portfolios are most common.)
- Recommendations needed
- Transcript requirements
- GPA
- Test scores
- CLEP/AP/DANTES accepted
- Scholarships (with URL links)
- Scholarship deadlines
- Additional considerations

Some parents and students have benefited from adding columns to record correspondence with colleges including when applications were filed and whether scholarship packages were accepted or declined.

In addition, walking on campus is an important part of college selection and affects students differently. Some young adults feel comfortable in a smaller, close-knit environment. Others love the excitement of a large sprawling university. If the student walks on campus and "feels at home," with a sense that the campus is the next right step into the future, he or she will be more likely to persevere through trials, remaining at the university through graduation.

If a high school student has a unique interest, parents can talk through the possibilities and encourage an online search for career options within the interest. While searching, one should make note of universities offering majors in that area of interest. If the student intends to pursue any unique profession, one offered at very few universities, it will be important to plan how the student will meet the admission requirements. With only one or two college choices, there will be little wiggle room when applying.

Unique Majors for Unique Interests

Engineering
- Arctic engineering
- Navel engineering
- Theme park engineering
- Geophysical engineering

Medical
- Integrative health sciences

Environmental
- Plant, soil, and insect studies
- Nautical archeology

Mathematical
- Logic

Business
- Cosmetic and fragrance marketing
- Leadership studies
- Decision sciences

Educational
- Children's literature

Art
- Puppetry
- Fibers
- Jewelry and metalsmithing

Music
- Pipe organ performance
- Tour production

Science
- Astrobiology
- Animal behavior

Agricultural
- Master ranching
- Animal behavior
- Farrier science

Law Enforcement
- Juvenile corrections
- Juvenile justice and advocacy
- Forensic photography

Food and Entertainment
- Meeting and event planning
- Food science
- Audio technology
- Game design
- Tour production
- Bakery science
- Bakery and pastry arts

Recreational
- Adventure education
- Recreation and leisure sciences

Sports
- Turfgrass management
- Golf management

Checking the scholarship requirements for the top colleges is also wise. Many colleges require specific courses, community service hours, grade point averages, and test scores, all of which must be submitted in order for the student to be considered. Knowing these requirements in advance help parents and students plan ahead, avoiding stress at submission time and possibly saving thousands of dollars.

The table on page 51 compares three universities as an example of how admission requirements can vary.* Understanding the variance can be a helpful tool for parents eager to help students achieve their goals.

Courses: Recommended or Required

At the end of my workshops I am frequently asked, "What high school courses do colleges recommend or require for admission?" The answer varies from college to college, often dependent on whether the college is public, private, non-competitive, highly selective, or somewhere in between. Though there are similarities, there are also differences. Some colleges list recommended courses for admission while others are specific about required courses with no substitutions. Parents and students should research and record findings on The Big Comparison list, especially for top colleges of choice. Reading wording on websites carefully can save stressful moments come application time.

There is a difference between recommend and require. Recommend means to strongly encourage. There may be some leeway if the student submits high test scores. For example, a student with a 1450 on the SAT may be able to get away with not taking a recommended physics course. On the other hand, if physics is listed as a required science, the college may not overlook the omission. If during The Big Comparison detailed on page 48 one finds that physics is required by three out of five top college choices, the student should seriously consider adding physics to the four-year high school plan. As the high school years roll along, the student may eliminate choices from the top college list and decide not to take physics if the colleges on the new top list are not requiring physics. The four-year plan can be changed with the understanding the college choices may be limited.

I appreciate the freedom of home education and the ability to accommodate learning styles and preferences of my children. However, I also realize I may have to help colleges understand the extraordinary learning opportunities we enjoy. In this process it is helpful for me to remember that most colleges view education from a traditional lens. Colleges with this viewpoint believe courses have specific standards to be met or content to be learned, generally with a textbook as a resource. They speak educationese.

To help colleges understand the caliber and depth of our home learning, I translate all the wonderful learning opportunities my high schoolers experience into the language and formats college officials understand. Many of the sections in this book—specifically credits, transcripts, and course titles and descriptions—offer our experiences or the experiences of other families as examples to help you translate the learning taking place in your home into terms and documents that colleges request.

Though our students may learn some subjects experientially through middle and high school, I understand I may have to translate our non-traditional learning into traditional paperwork. I try not to allow the fear of providing such documents to dictate or determine our content or methods. In other words, if we know our student learns best with experiential learning, we continue to incorporate those opportunities into the high school journey.

	Recommended High School Courses	Application Requirements	Homeschool Transcript Elements	Additional Considerations
Cedarville University (as of May 2015) https://www.cedarville.edu/Admissions/Home-Schooled-Students.aspx	• **4 units English** (grammar, composition, and literature) • **3-4 units math** (algebra I and II, geometry, and trigonometry) • **3 units natural science** (physical science, biology, and chemistry) • **3 units social studies** (history and government) • **2-3 units foreign language** (not ASL)	• Application for admission • High school transcript • College transcripts • Test scores (22 ACT; 1020 SAT) • GPA of 3.0 unweighted • Church leader recommendation	• Required with course titles, grades, credits, anticipated graduation date, and parent signature	
Emory University (as of May 2015) http://apply.emory.edu/apply/requirements.php		• All requirements for public and private school students and these additional: ⇒ Test scores from three additional SAT II tests (one math and two student choice) ⇒ Letter of recommendation from non-family member ⇒ Comprehensive explanation of the curriculum		• Artistically talented students who feel their accomplishments cannot be showcased on the Common Application may submit a supplemental arts information
Arizona State University (as of May 2015) https://students.asu.edu/freshman/requirements	• **4 years English** (composition/literature based) • **4 years math** (algebra I and II, geometry, and 1 year of Algebra II prerequisite math) • **3 years laboratory science** (earth science, biology, chemistry, physics, or integrated science) • **3 years social science** (1 year must be American history) • **2 years foreign language** • **1 year fine arts**	**Must meet one of the following :** ⇒ Top 25% of high school class ⇒ 3.00 GPA of competency courses ⇒ 22 ACT (24 non-residents) ⇒ 1040 SAT (1110 non-residents) *Writing portions of ACT and SAT not required *Met Competency Requirements * Complete Evaluation of Laboratory Sciences		

*These universities were chosen to give parents examples of how admission requirements can vary. Their inclusion is random. The author is not endorsing one university over another and there is no compensation being given for their mention in this publication.

Furthermore, if our high school student learns best by weaving content areas together in a seamless unit—as opposed to segmented subjects—we continue to integrate studies. In the end, the unique experiences our students enjoy prove best in terms of learning and have been the most significant and intriguing to employers and colleges.

In our college admission experiences, we found most colleges extremely cooperative, even welcoming of our coursework and paperwork. One admission advisor I spoke with assured me his university appreciated home education and was willing to work with home graduates. At the end of our phone conversation, he confidently stated, "Mrs. Bastian, I was homeschooled, and I understand it can be different. Submit the application paperwork, along with the student's transcript. We like homeschooled graduates and are willing to work with them." Within two weeks, our student received an acceptance letter. An application to the university's honors program followed a week later.

Knowing which courses could be recommended or required by potential employers and college admissions was helpful as we created four-year plans for our young adults. For courses which were most challenging for our students, I considered postponing study or finding alternatives for the course, in content or method. Before any final decisions were made as to whether we would eliminate a course required by several top choice colleges, my husband, I, and the student would process options as well as the consequences of forgoing a course. After home educating four high schoolers, my experience is that great growth and maturity can occur in the junior and senior year. I did not want our high school students short-changed or stressed when admission time rolled around. On the other hand, I also knew if a class was needed and the student was determined, it could be completed in less than a year because of the freedom homeschooling affords to learn anything at any given time, without a predetermined time frame.

Courses– The Content

Colleges expect certain courses be present on a transcript. The next several pages list the courses most often recommended or required for college-bound middle and high school students. Credit hours in parentheses are the hours a majority of colleges require. These are guidelines. One should always check the young adult's top colleges of choice to be sure the four-year plan includes the hours required for each college. It is helpful to remember four-for-sure: four credits in each of the core subjects—English, math, social science, and science—for most competitive universities.

Young adults have individual learning preferences. The bulleted lists offer examples of how homeschool families have fulfilled credits within each subject area. Home education offers freedom to use what works best for individual families, but when awarding credit, parents are reminded to be sure the content is high school level.

English (four high school credits)

- Colleges assume English study will consist of writing composition, literature analysis, grammar application, and vocabulary building.

- Colleges prefer students read genres from American, world, and British literature. Traditional high schools generally focus on one origination each year. During the fourth year of English study, students in some schools have the option of choosing literature of interest, perhaps contemporary, Shakespearean, Asian, or ancient literature. When my oldest son was in high school, I researched International Baccalaureate, Advanced Placement, Honors, and college preparatory literature. During my study, I compiled lists for my high schooler based on the origination of the piece or author. When he studied a specific historical period, he used the literature lists as a spring board to possible reading selections. The literature lists I compiled are included on page 102.

There is not a consistent progression plan for literature courses, meaning each school offers literature components during different years. Some home education families choose to weave literature with history studies creating many possible combinations of study dependent upon which history is selected.

Course*	Corresponding Social Science	Grade
English I/ American Literature (CLEP available)	American History	Grade 9
English I/World Literature (CLEP available)	World Geography & Cultures	Grade 9
English II/ Ancient World Literature	Ancient World History	Grade 10
English II/World Literature (CLEP available)	Modern World History	Grade 10
English II/ World Literature (CLEP available)	World History	Grade 10
English III/World Literature (CLEP available)	World History	Grade 11
English III/British Literature (CLEP available)	World History	Grade 11
English IV/ British Literature (CLEP available)	American Government & Economics	Grade 12
English IV/ Contemporary Literature (CLEP available)	American Government & Economics	Grade 12

* CLEP information current May 2015, check availability after this date.

- Parents can consider additional English credits for students who write for publication, attend writer workshops or literary presentations, or compete in state or national speech or debate competitions.

- Participating in book clubs, literary discussion groups, and writing cooperative classes can enhance English and literature studies for some young adults. Some parents and students have added these opportunities to courses.

A Reason to Celebrate

We chose to take a less traditional approach to literature study. Whereas high schools tend to segment literature studies into categories, we chose to let our student read freely from literature lists recommended for college-bound high schoolers. Some selections were hard copies and others digital. Once a selection was read, our student added the title to a reading list, one like Cheryl suggests on page 100. Though we learned more non-traditionally, I grouped literature selections categorically so colleges could better understand the scope of our student's reading. When I wrote course descriptions, which were required by several of the colleges to which we applied, I used Cheryl's literature lists to help me place the titles into literature courses recognized by colleges. I included the student's reading list in the college admission packet.

- Believing good writing is bred from reading excellent, vocabulary-rich literature, some homeschooling parents and students choose to earn English credits solely with substantial reading and writing.

- Writing may include practical, real-world opportunities: letters to editors, poetry and prose, admission and scholarship essays, plays and monologues, literary analysis, movie reviews, book proposals, emails, blog entries, and media captions.

- Research and study skills often proceed and accompany writing. These skills improve with practice. Some home educating parents find these skills are built most effectively as students research topics of interest versus "artificial" research papers.

- Vocabulary development may include the study of Greek and Latin roots.

- To enhance literature studies, families have visited the birthplaces and homesteads of famous authors. A short list of adventures appears on page 108.

- High school students with learning differences have used audio books, e-readers, voice-to-write programs or speech recognition applications, and online synopses as tools for greater understanding and retention.

A Reason to Celebrate

We chose a purposeful, practical approach for our daughter's twelfth grade writing component. Scholarship and college essays were a reality, especially in the beginning of the school year. In fact, it seemed we spent more time writing than anything else. Wanting to prepare her for college and knowing college English courses emphasize narrative, expository, and persuasive writing, we felt writing and editing essays was much more profitable than arbitrary assignments. Many of the essays also had to be precise, under a specified word count, which added another element to her assignments. Our daughter also created a resume for a job application, which we printed and placed it in her writing portfolio.

Mathematics (three high school credits, four high school credits for competitive or highly selective)

- Colleges look for math progression. In other words, the student is progressing—taking on more difficult math—each year. Most colleges expect students to have completed at least three credits, and often four, beginning with Algebra I and continuing to Geometry and Algebra II. The traditional progression varies from school to school.

Course*	Grade
General Math - Math 6, Math 7, Math 8	Grades 6-8
Pre-Algebra	Grades 7-9, usually grade 8 or 9
Algebra I	Grades 7-11, usually grade 9 or 10, complete before Chemistry
Consumer Math	Grades 9-12 , non-college bound
Business Math	Grades 9 - 12, non-college bound or elective
Algebra II	Grades 9 - 12, usually grade 11 or 12
Pre-Calculus (CLEP available)	Grades 10-12
Calculus (CLEP, AP Calculus AB and AP Calculus BC available)	Grades 11-12
Statistics (AP course available)	Grades 11-12, after two years of Algebra

*CLEP and AP information current May 2015, check availability after this date.

- Students aspiring to apply to highly selective colleges must pay close attention to the required math courses; usually four credits are needed. Advanced math courses—Calculus, Analytical Geometry and Trigonometry—may be expected.

- Parents may consider consumer math, business math, or personal finance as electives, even for college-bound students. These courses teach important consumer principles including insurance coverage (life, car, and home owners), salaries and taxes, budgeting, banking, investments, and small business skills. Practical applications such as couponing, comparison shopping, planning home improvement projects, opening and maintaining a check or savings account, applying for a credit card (to establish credit but paying off monthly), investing in real estate or stocks, purchasing a vehicle with applicable insurance, and filing appropriate taxes as an employee are also valuable.

- Math can coincide with career goals. Experiential learning and application to everyday life may make the difference in understanding mathematical concepts. A student running a business might have a natural interest in business math with complementary electives in personal finance or economics. Parents need to determine whether the young adult's practical learning is credit worthy.

Social Sciences (three high school credits, four high school credits for competitive or highly selective colleges)

- Traditionally colleges look for credits in American and world history, American government, and economics. The credit awarded to American government and economics may be a half credit or a full credit pending the amount of time the student spends studying and learning. Progression varies school to school; there is a trend to place American government and economics in the senior year as economic concepts can be complicated and require additional math skills. CLEP and AP tests must be taken to receive credit.

Course*	Grade
World Geography	Grades 9 or 10
Human Geography (AP course available)	Grades 9 or 10
American History may be divided into two years (CLEP and AP courses available)	Grades 9 - 12
World History may be divided into two years (CLEP and AP courses available)	Grades 9 - 12
European History (AP course available)	Grades 10-12
American Government (CLEP and AP courses available)	Grades 9 - 12
Economics (AP course available)	Grades 9 -12, usually grade 12
Psychology (CLEP and AP courses available)	Grade 12
Human Growth and Development (CLEP available)	Grade 12
Sociology (CLEP and AP courses available)	Grade 12

* CLEP and AP information current May 2015, check availability after this date.

- Some families chose to divide American History into two years (two credits) - American History: Colonization to 1865 and American History: 1865 to Present. They may do the same with World History - World History: Ancient to Reformation and World History: Reformation to Present. This allows each year to be studied in depth, incorporating literature pieces, biographies, and primary source documents. If the student intends to take corresponding CLEP exams, one should adjust time periods to correspond with material covered on this assessment.

- Experiential learning opportunities in state government or service in the senate page program are valuable and allow the student to stand out among other applicants. Consider observing school, city, county, or state council and board meetings as well. Students we know with an interest in government and law have earned credit for serving in peer positions with juvenile court or participating in political campaigns. These opportunities are especially valuable for students interested in law or political careers.

- Social sciences lend well to non-traditional learning. Some students have toured historical landmarks and museums, visited national parks and government buildings, read biographies and primary source documents, listened to audio books, participated in historical reenactments, created timelines to enhance studies, initiated independent studies, and studied family genealogy, interviewing relatives about the history in their lifetimes.

- Imagine studying history from an object of interest. Some students have successfully studied history as related to fabrics, toys, holidays, stamps, industry, art, instruments, cooking, and beverages. There is history in every interest and students may be more enthused about learning history related to something they enjoy. Some families take a break—days, weeks, or even a month—from traditional studies to dig deeper into an area of intrigue.

- There are a plethora of options available to home educated students in the areas of social sciences. Psychology, sociology, humanities, Russian history, ancient history, archeology, European geography, and anthropology are wonderful course options for students with interest in these areas or for those seeking admission into highly selective colleges. Career decisions may also be determined by these studies.

Science (three credits, two of which include laboratory studies; four credits for science majors or competitive colleges)

- College requirements for science can vary greatly. Some colleges will not require labs. Others, like Arizona State University, require applicants to submit an Evaluation of Laboratory Sciences form validating the comprehensiveness of the lab portion of the course.

- Many colleges require the three credits to be earned: biology, chemistry, and physics. Other colleges appreciate students who have completed unique, area specific courses such as botony, zoology, geology, equine science, nutrition, and astronomy. Researching college admission requirements for science is vital for students anticipating medical or animal science careers and seeking admission to highly selective colleges.

- Some students choose to learn science with practical experiences: working at a botanical garden, participating in classes at a local science center, volunteering at an animal hospital or clinic, visiting museums, working at a horse farm, working on a sod farm, or competing in a local science fair or 4H competition. Often gardens, parks, libraries, zoos, and colleges offer summer enrichment classes. Inquire about high school classes at these sites.

Parents should research employment and college admission requirements to be sure mandatory sciences are added to the student's four year high school plan.

Course	Grade
Physical Science	Grades 8 or 9
Biology (CLEP and AP courses available)	Grades 9 or 10
Marine Biology	Grades 9 - 12
Environmental Science (AP course available)	Grades 10 - 12
Chemistry (CLEP and AP courses available)	Grades 9 - 12
Physics (AP course available)	Grades 10 - 12
Human Anatomy and Physiology	Grades 11 - 12

* CLEP and AP information current May 2015, check availability after this date.

Foreign Language (two credits, same language, two consecutive years)

• Highly selective colleges may require three or four years of language.

Learn from Our Mistake

We did not know. We learned the hard way and want others to consider our experience so they do not hit the road block we encountered.

We made sure our student had two years of foreign language. Done. So, what was the problem? When we went to apply for our merit scholarship, we found out the our student was disqualified because there was a semester break in the middle of his two-year study of foreign language. The two years were not consecutive.

Be sure to check wording for scholarships and college admission carefully. If the requirements state consecutive, take one class right after the other.

- American Sign Language is accepted as a foreign language—sometimes called world languages— by some colleges but not by others. Parents should double-check with colleges of choice to confirm ASL acceptance.

- Families have found this requirement situation specific. If there is doubt as to what a college or scholarship will accept or require, one should ask questions before course study is started. Some families make sure correspondence is in writing to avoid a discrepancy later.

A Reason to Celebrate

Our sons completed Spanish I and II through our state virtual school. The oldest enrolled in a four-year state university. The university asked for verification of his two years of high school foreign language which was provided by the state virtual school. Not only did the university approve the high school credits, but they also waived the college foreign language graduation requirement because the credits were earned through the state virtual school. Our younger son enrolled in the state college. They, too, asked for verification of the credits by means of my transcript, as well as the state virtual school transcript, and waived the foreign language requirement for his Associates in Arts degree. After earning his degree, my son transferred to a state university. The school asked me to submit his final high school transcript to verify high school foreign language completion through an acceptable means. Two weeks later, my son received a letter waiving the graduation requirement for his bachelor's degree— a definite savings.

Electives

Electives are often natural extensions of integrating life and learning, giving students the opportunity to gain skills and understanding in many areas. Electives also offer employers and college admission officials an intriguing glimpse of the unique studies of the student. It is the extraordinary electives which often allow the student to stand out among other perspective employees or applicants.

Though electives most often reference courses in the areas of music, visual and fine arts, driver's education, health and nutrition, and physical education, there are situations where core courses become electives—commonly referred to as academic electives. When students complete the required number for courses in a core content area—perhaps biology, marine biology, chemistry, and physics—and then decide to take or dual enroll another course, maybe human anatomy, one of the classes may be considered an academic elective. Some students pursue extra courses in a core area due to interest. Others choose this academic path hoping to increase the likelihood of being offered admission in a highly selective college.

Electives allow a student the flexibility to investigate career fields of interest before entering the workforce or seeking college admission. For example, a student contemplating a career in health sciences dual enrolls Introduction to Health Sciences through the local state college. Taking the course, the student discovers she has a more specific interest in pediatric dentistry and decides to job shadow with a pediatric dentist. She spends a total of 100 hours at the office observing the interactions between dentist and patients in a variety of situations, watches dental procedures, and helps dental assistants refill supplies. While job shadowing she talks with the dentist and hygienist about their and career paths. As a complement to her experiential learning, the student researches colleges offering her major and writes a research paper on current practices in pediatric dentistry. Her mom titles this elective course Introduction to Pediatric Dentistry. This young lady will likely catch the attention of college admissions, first for her interest in health sciences and second because she initiated steps toward solidifying her intent to pursue pediatric dentistry.

Parents often ask me how they should determine elective courses for their high school students. The answers vary. There is not one pat answer suitable to meet the needs of all students. If there was, local public and private schools would not be offering such a great variety of electives in an effort to satisfy the broad range of student interest. Home education has the potential to offer students an unlimited selection of elective courses.

To determine which electives might be best for our student during the high school years, we ponder important questions:

- Where does our student spend his or her extra time?

Experiential learning cannot be discounted. In fact, studies show that hands-on, mind-engaged purposeful learning is effective. Observe what the student is already doing: taking music lessons, volunteering at a hospital, working with children with learning challenges, recording music or vocal performances, researching a topic, or building inventory for a business. Consider whether the activities the student is already engaged in is worthy of credit. Some are and some are not.

- Is there enough time spent on concentrated learning to consider awarding credit for a course?

We found the answer to this question are very important. The colleges our student applied to wanted to know how our student spent his or her discretionary time while in high school. If our student spent significant time in one area and learned the material at or above high school level, we had the ability per our state statute, to decide whether to award credit to those efforts. In doing so, and in titling the course accurately to reflect the material, colleges learned about our student.

- What work or volunteer experience has sparked an interest in our student?

Our daughter enjoys children, and she is extremely gifted in her interactions and care of them. When she expressed interest in getting a job, we suggested asking the director at a local preschool if there was a job opening for a teacher's assistant. There was and she began working two days a week. Her interest grew. She read the child development manual given to teachers and observed several different types of parenting styles. On her own initiative, she read a book about how the parent-child relationship affects infant and child development. When the school year ended our daughter began working with older children at a summer art camp. As her interest for child development grows and she continues to learn or work in this area with quality mentors, we will consider awarding her high school credit for her efforts.

- What interest does our student have that has not been investigated? What would the student want to explore more in-depth?

Students often have interests they do not feel they have time to pursue. Keeping hands open to opportunities and possibilities within a potential area of study allows the student a chance to evaluate priorities and schedules. In processing thoughts and ideas, the student may realize there is not only time but also potential for volunteer work, community service, and even employment in the area of interest. Learning springs forth from these options. Thankfully, homeschooling offers the freedom to learn more, dig deeper, and investigate further.

Perhaps a young adult wants to learn more about ornithology, the study of birds. He states that there has not been time to pursue the interest. A discussion with the student reveals there is not only time—since there are less important activities eating up the schedule—but also resources in the local area to make the study possible. From the discussion, an initial plan is created: use SORA (Searchable Ornithology Research Archive) to access ornithological publications for research and study, enter the research project in the AMNH Naturalist Awards, find out information about the Association of Field Ornithologists, visit the local Audubon Society center, learn about James Audubon by reading a biography, research possible local birding activities by searching "local birding in (city or state name)" and participate in one. From these ideas, others may grow and the parent may decide to award credit based on the depth of study.

Although electives similar to what a traditional high school offers are best understood by college administrators, it does not mean outside the box electives are not acceptable. In fact, it is the unique which will intrigue college admissions personnel. Parents must carefully assist colleges in understanding the scope and depth of courses should questions be asked in an interview or course descriptions be requested. A detailed explanation of course description writing begins on page 75.

After a parent discovers possible elective course options for a student, the next question that follows is, "How do I know what to include in the course so it counts as credit?" I have asked the same question, especially for unconventional courses, elective or academic core. The first thing I do is remind myself that according to our state home education statute, I am the overseer of the education of my children. I have the right, freedom, and responsibility to determine what content makes up a course and what credit to award, but I must be able to validate my decision should university personnel request. I must also know how many hours generally constitute a credit (see page 70) and then oversee the completion of the required hours.

The second step I take is to search online for course syllabi or descriptions with titles or content similar to what my student has done or is considering. For instance, my state high school course offerings have given me ideas for content. In fact, most states post course requirements for their high school offerings online. At the same time, the high school course does not have to be offered in my state. If I cannot find an equivalent or appropriate high school level course, I search for similar college course syllabi and descriptions.

If you are homeschooling in the state of Florida, check this link for options.

⌨ http://www.cpalms.org/Public/search/Course#0

Home educators often learn comprehensively through life experiences and opportunities. Often times the learning must be "dissected" in order to award credit and title courses in a manner employers or colleges will understand. For example, private music instruction generally includes music theory but might also incorporate music history and appreciation. When titling courses, consult high school courses offered by the state or look over the list on page 87.

Elective Subject Area	Potential Content Areas
Music	Private instruction, performance, theory, composition, appreciation, and history
Visual Arts	Private instruction in technique and media (drawing, painting, multi-media, 3-D art sculpture, photography) and appreciation
Performing Arts	Private instruction (ballet, dance, and vocal), theater and drama
Health and Nutrition	Personal fitness, personal training, nutrition, first aid, emergency preparedness, health care, food preparation (cake decorating, specialty menus) and cultural cuisine
Clothing and Textiles	Sewing and quilting instruction, fashion and interior design
Driver's Education	Traffic safety, signage, and practice
Physical Education	Team and recreational sports

Driver's and physical education courses are not always considered electives.

Elective credits may be earned through shadowing and interning. The high school years are ideal for young adults to gain experiential knowledge in an occupational field of interest; enabling the student to gain understanding as to whether a field may be suitable as a future career. For example, if a young adult anticipates pursuing a degree in veterinary medicine, finding a veterinarian to shadow, interview, and discuss educational options with will be extremely valuable. These opportunities allow the student to learn from professionals in the job setting, facing real-life scenarios. The experience also provides opportunity for the high schooler to observe interactions between the medical professional and patients or employees. In this situation, the parent and student decide how to the experiential knowledge gained will be integrated into course descriptions, noted on transcripts, or documented on college applications.

Although some colleges require specific courses, there are also colleges seeking students who have distinctive interests, talents, and successes. Business and patent owners, state champions, community leaders, and published authors make significant contributions to a college campus or community.

A Reason to Celebrate

Our daughter was interested in swimming and loved the beach, so it seemed natural for her to become involved in the junior lifeguard program. She became certified as a lifeguard as well as in scuba. We counted both of these accomplishments toward her physical education credits. In addition, we added this information to her extracurricular resume because it showed another aspect to our daughter's interests, painting a more defined picture of a young adult who was not afraid of challenges and strenuous physical activity. She worked diligently to attain her goals and was able to follow through to achieve certification. We wanted the college to know who our daughter is and what she would bring to the university.

Test Scores

Aside from the transcript, test scores can be the most unnerving requirement for college admission. Parents often share this anxiety with me when I meet with them. Indeed, test scores have been a growing concern in the past few years, a fear which is driving homeschooling parents to test children earlier to "be sure" their one-day-young-adults will be ready for their college entrance exams. As a parent of past, current, and upcoming high schoolers, I understand.

The fear of testing is real. Often scores determine college admission for competitive colleges or scholarship awards. In addition, for some colleges, scores on the SAT, SAT II subject tests, or ACT are more important for the homeschooled student than for their public or private schooled competitors. Additionally, some colleges often require more testing, usually SAT II subject tests, from homeschooled applicants. So, there is merit behind the concern. However, many universities are now recognizing that testing is not necessarily an accurate indicator of college success or completion.

When comparing the admission requirements for top colleges of choice, note the test score requirements. If the school requires one test over another, meet that requirement, if the student is able and willing. If not, seek other options. When a school specifies a test, walk alongside your student, helping him or her to understand the format, scope, and content of the test.

Taking practice tests can be valuable, especially if the test setting is recreated. Taking the test multiple times, using a timer and at the same time of the day the actual test will be administered helps the student acclimate to the test format, questions, and timing. In addition, test objectives vary, therefore different study techniques and test-taking strategies are needed for each test. Knowing this, the student has a greater chance for testing success.

Some colleges and universities, realizing testing is not the only indicator of academic success, are trending toward becoming test-optional or flexible. For example, Furman University in South Carolina is a test-optional school (referenced May 2015). That being the case, Furman does require homeschooled students to complete a phone interview with their homeschool coordinator. Families who are curious about test-optional educational venues should search "test-optional universities" online.

When a college superscores a test, admissions personnel take the highest math, critical reading, and writing subscores the student submitted and adds the subscores to get an overall higher score. Not every school superscores all tests, so it is important to find out whether a prospective school does or does not. For example, Bowdoin college is one school which accepts superscoring for the SAT, but not for the ACT.

Placement exams are tests required before class registration to determine what courses the student can take and complete successfully. If the student does not attain the minimum score on the placement test, the college will require the student to take an intermediate or remedial class before taking freshman level courses. Placement exams are common at state colleges in the areas of English, math, and science. The test is often not timed—a good option for some students.

Advanced Placement (AP) exams are the culmination of a one-year AP course on a specific subject. Each college or university decides how credit will be awarded based on a minimum score they determine. The courses and tests are most often taken in the junior year. Some colleges prefer AP credit over dual enrollment as AP courses and exams are standardized. Other colleges require them for admission, especially highly selective colleges. As with any aspect of college admission, be sure to check the requirements of the student's colleges of choice.

> The college board created a page specific to homeschooled students taking AP tests.
> 🖳 http://professionals.collegeboard.com/testing/ap/scores/prepare/homeschool

The College-Level Examination Placement (CLEP) exam is another common test taken prior to college admission. These tests offer the young adult an opportunity to earn college credit. CLEP does not require the completion of a specific course, though it is wise to use CLEP study tools prior to testing.

Though testing and earning college credit has become more popular, not all colleges and universities accept every test. Also, some schools do not accept dual enrollment—some courses transfer easily, others do not. This is another reason why making a comparable list of top college choices is so important. Though testing out of college credit can be cost effective in some situations, this is not always the case. Before spending money on testing, thinking it will boost acceptance potential or lessen the time spent on postsecondary education, research first. Additional information on testing can be found on page 122.

Extracurricular Activities

The more unique and intriguing, the better when it comes to extracurricular activities. Extracurriculars tell college and universities about the student, specifically, how they managed their free time. In fact, extracurricular activities can boost a student's ranking when compared to other applicants. Al Nunez, Director of Admissions, at Illinois Institute of Technology, interviewed for the November 13, 2014 issue of *U. S. News and World Report*, whereby he encouraged students when "to brag about themselves, explaining all the things they have done, including jobs, volunteer work, and community service." The article can be read at the link below.

> 🖳 http://www.usnews.com/education/best-colleges/articles/2013/11/12/incorporate-jobs-hobbies-into-college-applications

Extracurricular achievements make excellent topics for college application essays. Through the essay, colleges and universities come to know the student, their strengths, how they have impacted their communities, and what they will bring to the campus. Extracurricular activities in conjunction with student essays give admissions personnel a thorough, holistic understanding of who the student is and what the student will bring to the campus.

Colleges are fond of activities which denote a student committed long-term to an activity, exhibited leadership or service, pursued intellectual or personal growth outside of coursework, impacted the community, or used communication, cooperation, and collaboration skills with other participants. These activities are often not highlighted anywhere else in the application packet. Keeping track of your young adult's extracurricular activities, including the positions of leadership held in those activities, the scope of service opportunities, and the number of hours spent in each activity, may pay off when the time comes to apply for college admission and scholarships.

A Reason to Celebrate

Our daughter is what we call "gifted with a glitch." She is very bright and does well in school. She also has dyslexia, dysgraphia, and a processing disorder. You would never know she faces these obstacles by speaking with her or following her around. One can only see her challenges when reviewing her writing. As a result of her learning disabilities, our daughter decided not to take the SAT or ACT. She was excited to discover her first choice in college was a test-optional school.

Test optional schools want to know more about the student, so we submitted her extracurricular activities. She had logged over 2,000 hours of community service in her high school years and participated in a wide variety of other activities: community choir, speech and debate, 4-H, mission trips, the Senate Page program, art classes, and acting in a Shakespeare group. It was never our interest to do what we thought would look good on her transcript, but instead to do what she was interested in doing or things related to what we were studying.

When applying to Stetson University, our daughter was viewed as a very well-rounded individual based on her strong academic transcript and extracurricular activities. She was offered admission with a full scholarship. She also awarded the Bonner scholarship, a scholarship offered to students involved in community service, eager to continue helping others while in college. In addition to a full-time load, she must keep up her GPA, volunteer ten hours a week at an area charity, and volunteer for two summers of service. This summer she is serving poor children in New Zealand.

Our daughter did not volunteer in high school because she was looking for a scholarship. Volunteering was what we did as a family. In the end, however, our daughter was blessed to be rewarded a free education based on her interests and her heart for serving others.

The Personal Interview

Personal interviews provide a means for college admission personnel to get to know students better. Colleges are now using interviews to determine candidacy for admission as well as determination of scholarship. This bodes well for home educated students who are generally comfortable with adult conversation.

Our son received a letter of candidacy for the Presidential Scholarship at two highly selective schools. As a candidate for the scholarship, our son was required to attend a personal interview with the college president. Knowing colleges are utilizing this means to get to know students better, if your young adult is uncomfortable with an interview process, make a list of potential interview questions and role play. This list may help jump start a brainstorming session:

- Tell me about yourself.
- Why are you interested in attending (name of school)?
- What is your intended major?
- Why have you chosen (major) as your intended major?
- Why do you look forward to attending (name of school)?
- How will you contribute to or impact our campus?
- Who has most impacted your life? How?

The interviewer may also ask the student if he has any questions about the university. Well-thought-out questions inform the interviewer that the student took time to research the college. If the student does research and prepares a few questions in advance, he is less likely to be caught off-guard and will be able to participate in a meaningful conversation.

The Admissions Packet

Items required in an admissions packet will vary from college to college. Almost all colleges request a transcript, while only a few may request a student's reading list. This component could be added to The Big Comparison list (page 47). Regardless of what documents are required, the goal is to give a college or university a holistic presentation of the student. Colleges may require the following items:

- Transcript (page 90) or home education completion affidavit
- A student resume
- Course descriptions (page 75) and assignments
- Reading list (page 100)
- Documentation or verification of scientific laboratory work (common in Arizona)
- Documentation of community service venues and hours
- Letters of recommendation from significant people in the student's life (page 114)

When we were ready to submit our application packet, I called the college to be sure the documents would be sent to the right individual. Some colleges now have designated admissions advisors for homeschooled applicants. This is especially true of colleges seeking students from the homeschool community.

A Reason to Celebrate

In our experience, the admission packet — course descriptions, reading list, and community service log — confirmed our student was more than a test score. The packet narrowed the gap between her test scores and her strengths. Our student had her own business, was honored with leadership awards in sports, and had accumulated a significant number of community service hours. None of these impressive traits could be communicated in test scores but were able to be documented in the admission packet. The student was accepted to the college of her choice and awarded third place for a Christian Leadership Scholarship.

To our surprise, the high school paperwork we kept for her admission to college became the core of her first resume. The resume, in turn, opened up career opportunities, including a one semester nanny position in Italy and European travel. When she applied to be a parent at an international boarding school, her European nanny and travel experience provided a competitive edge over a college-degreed Residential Assistant with one year experience. Our daughter was offered the position. Experiential learning has been essential in the educational and employment opportunities presented to our daughter.

Notes

Chapter 7

High School Record Keeping

Record keeping has saved my high school mom sanity! Seriously. Though the records take time to keep, when time rolled around and I needed important documents they were ready. Well, maybe not always ready, but at least in good enough shape that I could fine tune a few sentences and click print. How did I get to that place? Not by accident; only with intentionality.

The Annual High School Portfolio

At the beginning of a new school year, I give our high school students a four-inch, three-ring binder stocked with tab dividers and plastic document sleeves. Our students label the tabs with current course titles. As course work is completed, it is our students' responsibility to file papers behind the labeled dividers. Items which are not "three-ring friendly" are placed in plastic document sleeves. This method is similar to the portfolio I kept for my children in the lower grades.

Record Keeping Tip

What work samples are kept in a high school portfolio?

The purpose of the portfolio is to verify course content, record the progress of the student, and verify course hours, if needed. Work samples vary from course to course. Math samples might include problems from the lessons, scratch work, and tests. Science work samples may include lab reports, assignments, photos of dissections, and tests. Research papers, writing assignments, study guides, magazine articles, interviews, book critiques, theater tickets, and primary source documents are also important. If the student aspires to attend art school an additional art portfolio may be required for admission.

Cumulative high school records are kept in a separate three-ring binder. The paperwork and test results in this portfolio will help write supporting documents needed for employment or college admission (page 96).

Our state requires home education families to keep a log of activities. We prefer weekly logs, which I keep for the younger children. As the student matures and becomes independent, he or she is responsible to keep track of activities and completed assignments. I work with each student to find a method that will return the greatest chance for success.

Our first student kept his weekly logs (page 74) in the very front of the portfolio. He would mark subjects as he worked and listed books he was reading at the bottom of the page. I would check every few weeks to be sure the logs were being kept. This system worked well for him and at the end of the year I had the completed logs as easy references for course work hours, textbook titles, literature pieces, and community services hours.

Awarding Credits

Fifteen years ago when I attended my very first homeschooling high seminar one of the most surprising facts I learned was that there is not a uniform number of instructional and work hours designated to one credit hour. Some schools award one credit for 120 hours of work, while others award one credit for as many as 180 hours. I thought one credit hour was consistently the same, school to school, state to state; not the case. As a former educator and a home education mom looking ahead to the high school journey, I found this a helpful tidbit of information.

The most common method of awarding credits is the Carnegie Unit. One unit or credit is given for a course meeting thirty-six weeks, five days a week, for forty-five minutes each day, for a total of 120 hours. These hours are considered instructional hours. Additional study time is assumed.

High school textbooks for core subjects—English, math, social sciences, and natural sciences—are written as a full credit courses. Full credit courses are award one credit hour. In other words, the content included is assumed to take approximately thirty-six weeks to complete. Students who complete the class are awarded one credit, regardless of the number of study hours completed outside the class. Most academic classes—English, math, social sciences, natural sciences and foreign language—require a full school year to complete and are awarded one credit. Electives are generally half-credit courses, completed in one semester.

Though it is helpful to know how traditional credit is awarded, home education often utilizes a tutorial model of education. Instruction is concentrated, sometimes individualized, and greatly depends on the student's mastery of the material. Credits are often awarded differently in the tutorial setting, including both instruction, individual study, and experiential learning opportunities.

I am not advocating home educated students work less hours to obtain credit. Honestly, we always aim above the minimum standard. I encourage parents to understand the methodology behind determining credits as well as the role mastery plays in the tutorial model so they can make the best possible decisions regarding a student's education.

Using the Carnegie method as a guide, home education parents can tailor course content to the interests of the students. Students have earned high school credit with a plethora of options. The spectrum of possible scenarios depends on the interests and giftedness of the student, the course content, and the resources used. For example, there are many means by which a home education student could complete a high school biology course.

- **Scenario 1:** The student completed all lessons, lab experiences, and tests in a traditional high school level biology textbook. The parent awarded the student one credit.

- **Scenario 2:** An academically-talented student completed all the lessons, labs, and tests in a traditional high school level biology textbook. In addition, the student read *Reasonable Faith: The Scientific Case for Christianity* by Dr. Jay L. Wile, visited a biology lab at a local aquarium, and wrote a research paper on Darwin's theory of evolution. The parent awarded one credit because the student was capable of the additional work.

- **Scenario 3:** The student participated in a biology class taught by a former biology teacher and offered by a local homeschool cooperative. The student completed all class requirements including course work, dissections, and lab experiences, and an opportunity to teach science to elementary-age students. The teacher graded the work which was kept in a notebook. The parent awarded one credit.

- **Scenario 4:** The student studied in a biology lab at a local university. At the lab, the student participated in research projects, conducted independent studies, and discussed research results with the director of the biology department. The student was awarded Distinguished Student for his work. The parent awarded the student one credit.

- **Scenario 5:** The student enrolled in an online, accredited Honors Biology 101 course, completing all required assignments. The online academy awarded the student one honors credit on an official transcript which was submitted with the parent-generated transcript for college admission.

- **Scenario 6:** The student completed Biology 1011 in one semester through dual enrollment at a local community college. The college awarded the student three college credits, equivalent to one high school credit.

A Reason to Celebrate

One thing that stuck out to us was the fact that you stressed tailoring your child's high school years according to their interests. We really took this to heart. With both our girls having a heart for missions, we were able to tailor not only Bible, but history, science, and our fine arts around their interest and calling. The course description examples and book list in your book allowed us to get an idea how to write this to look professional and inspiring.

Designing High School Courses

Home educated students have many options for obtaining high school credit. Classes do not have to follow the same instructional format as traditional classroom courses. One class may be effectively taught with a textbook while another warrants a group laboratory setting. A variety of learning models can be used, giving the home education student a distinct educational advantage.

I designed courses for my high school students based on interest and learning style using a variety of opportunities. As I did, I was mindful of the traditional method of awarding credits.

- Traditional textbooks
- Primary source documents and literary works
- Lab experiences
- Independent study
- CD/DVD supplemental material and tutorials
- Co-curricular activities
- Travel opportunities
- Hobbies
- Tutors
- Volunteer opportunities
- Apprenticeships or internships
- Online classes (FLVS, PA Homeschoolers, Thomas Edison College)
- Dual enrollment
- AP/CLEP/DANTES testing

A Reason to Celebrate

Parents of artistic children often feel ill-equipped when it comes to preparing their students for a future career. When my daughter expressed interest in a non-traditional field I began searching for alternative ways to help her hone her craft. It was during this process we discovered a community of mentors, classes, and opportunities to help teach her during her high school years.

Art, like many creative fields, requires a different type of course planning. For this reason, we sought successful artists who had a passion to mentor younger artists. These seasoned creatives served as personal coaches. In the process she learned which types of mediums she preferred. My daughter learned valuable lessons from professionals who understood and could impart knowledge regarding the business side of her field. She acquired techniques she would latter practice in her studio. In addition, she cultivated connections with show directors, event planners, gallery and art supply owners, learning how to apply for shows and what pitfalls to avoid. These insights coupled with allowing her time to develop her craft paved the way for J. Albers Studio. What began in 2009 with photography expanded in 2013 to include fine art and design. Jeannie's creative process now involves multiple artistic mediums, combining elements of surrealism and imagination. Though her studio is located in Orlando, Florida, she searches for beauty everywhere, frequently traveling to photograph new people and places or sometimes just for the sake of adventure.

Documenting Hours

Mike and I sit with our students each year to develop an academic plan. Some years our planning is very formal, other years our planning is an informal discussion in the living room. Together we—Mike, I, and the student—decide which courses will be taken, how the courses will be taught, and how much credit the courses will be awarded. Traditional classes like algebra generally follow the lessons in the text. Other courses may follow a non-traditional approach. For some classes I designed a master assignment sheet. For other classes the student develops a plan to complete the course. No matter which approach is adopted, we make sure everyone, parents and student, are in agreement with course expectations.

If a class includes outside activities—labs, tours, interviews, job experiences, art training, or private instruction—we add those opportunities to our family calendar. Our next step is to create a weekly log for each student. Course titles are listed along with textbooks, resources, and additional reading materials. The student uses this log, similar to the one on page 74, to record the time spent on each subject.

Planning ahead allows us to estimate the number of hours the student will spend on each course. We make adjustments as necessary, adding assignments or experiences to equal the instructional hours needed for the credit we anticipate awarding. For courses which do not easily translate to an hourly requirement, for example small engine repair, we do our best to make sure the content is high school level and worthy of the credit awarded.

Sometimes we cannot estimate the number of hours a student will need to complete a course. In those cases, we record the hours the student worked on the weekly log and total the hours at the end of the course. Once the hours were totaled, we assigned credit.

Students accomplish educational goals differently. One of our students used a block schedule to plan his week. Instead of completing one hour of math, each day, five times a week, he worked on algebra for three hours on Monday and two hours on Tuesday. Wednesday and Thursday he would work on biology for two and one-half hours each day. On Friday, he took a break from algebra and biology to read literature. He decided how to manage his time to complete the requirements for his other classes. As he worked, he recorded his study hours on his weekly log. He had created his schedule and it was a perfect schedule for him, though it would not have been how I would have planned his time.

Our second high school student used a traditional schedule with the goal of working on each core subject, every day. He fit his elective studies around his core courses. My third high school student learns in chunks. She prefers to immerse herself in one subject for a concentrated amount of time until she completes the work or studies to the depth of her interest, sometimes at a post high school level. Though different in their approaches, all students were successful in completing their work.

Families document hours according to their organizational preferences. Our family recorded hours on our weekly log as explained in the above paragraphs. Logging hours was especially helpful for non-traditional courses and elective classes. Other families we know chose to document hours using a computer program, a check-off system, individual course spreadsheets, or a labeled 3x5 card system. There are also online programs available as well. It may be helpful to ask other parents and students what they use to log their study. The secret is finding a method which works for the student. If it works for the student, the hours will be recorded consistently and accurately.

Understanding the Role of Course Descriptions

States have detailed standards for the courses they offer. Core courses are offered in high schools across the United States and college admissions personnel are often familiar with standard requirements. However, classes taught at home generally differ from traditional classes in

Weekly Log
Student Name 2015-2016

Week of _Sept. 3-Sept. 9_

		M	T	W	Th	F	S	S
Advanced Mathematics	(1.0)	1.0	.75	1.0				
Human Anatomy and Physiology	(1.0)				.75	1.5		
Spanish 1*	(1.0)	1.0	1.0		1.0	1.0		
English IIII/ British Literature	(1.0)	.75	.75	.75	.75	1.0	1.0	
American Government	(0.5)		.50	.50	.50			
Business Systems Technology *	(0.5)	1.0		1.0	1.0			
SAT Prep*	(0.5)		.75			1.0		
Team Sports	(0.5)	2.0	2.5	3.0	3.0	2.0	2.0	

*(Student name) enrolled in online courses through _____School. Courses taken during the 2015-2016 school year: Spanish I, Basic Systems Technology and SAT Prep.

Textbooks Used:

Advanced Mathematics, John H. Saxon, Jr., Saxon Publishers, Inc., 2003

The Human Body: Fearfully and Wonderfully Made!, Dr. Jay Wile and Marilyn M. Shannon, Apologia Educational Ministries, 2001

Write for College, Patrick Sebranek, Verne Meyer and Dave Kemper, Write Source, Great Source Education Group, Houghton Mifflin, 1997

Introduction to English Literature, Jan Anderson and Laurel Hicks, A Beka Book Publishers, 1982

American Government in Christian Perspective, Bowen, Thompson, Lowman, and Cochran, 1997

Constitutional Law for Christian Students, Michael Farris, Esq., Home School Legal Defense Association, 1998.

Other Books:

The Innocence of Father Brown, G.K. Chesterton

A Year with C.S. Lewis: Daily Readings from His Classic Works, C. S. Lewis

Field Trips/Special Events

swimming and weights at YMCA, baseball practice , community service– 3hours OCC methodology, structure and content giving college administrators no standard for evaluation. For this reason, college admissions personnel considering home educated students for admission welcome—and sometimes require—course descriptions to accompany transcripts. These descriptions allow the college personnel to become familiar with the student and his or her interests.

Course descriptions serve two purposes. First, course descriptions clarify and validate course content. This is especially true when applying to universities which refuse to accept parent-granted honors credit. Once an admissions officer reads a course description, determination can be made as to whether the content is equivalent to a traditional honors level course and meets university expectations. Our oldest son faced this scenario.

*Please note: If you label a course "HONORS" be knowledgeable about the requirements for an honors level course and have the student exceed those standards. The education you offer at home will not be credible if your course titles do not reflect the course content.

Course descriptions also validate a student's academic abilities and achievements. Grades given by a parent on a transcript are occasionally considered suspect by college officials. However, when an admissions counselor compares course content to grades conferred on a transcript there may be a greater appreciation for the student's academic abilities and character. Students who submit a course description document at the time of application—even if the college did not request it—are often offered scholarship money, money that may not have been considered if the admissions office had received only a transcript.

The format we used can be found on page 84. I created this format based on what I would have had to provide for the NCAA if my son played collegiate sports. In addition, one highly selective school our first son applied to asked that specific student information be placed on the bottom of each page. I suspect this was requested so pages could be thumbed through quickly. This is likely no longer necessary as most documents are now digital. The point is, be mindful of requests made by your student's top college choices so you can follow their instructions and meet their requirements.

Our completed course description document for our first son was ten pages long in 11pt font. I placed like courses together in the same order as presented on the transcript: English courses first, math courses second, natural science courses third, social sciences fourth, and foreign (world) languages fifth, followed by electives. The descriptions captured concisely the significant content of the course. They were not entire syllabi.

Writing Course Descriptions

Course descriptions are "chapters" in your student's high school story. There are two main characters: your student and the courses. To write an accurate, unique story which jumps off the page and into the mind of a college administrator, you must know your characters. Take time to get to know the characters, documenting details, and effectively communicating your thoughts on paper. The results will be a story which will command a second read.

- **The Student**

Think about your student. What makes your student exceptional? What are your student's distinguishing traits? How is your student different from other students? What qualities are displayed in your student's work? What are your student's character qualities? The answers determine which courses your student will take, how the courses will be taught, and how the course will be described.

With these answers and descriptive words, you can describe your student within the context of a completed course. For example, when writing a course description for Advanced Flight Instruction, you could state "by the end of this course the student became a licensed pilot in a (specific type of aircraft)." Using correct terminology to describe your student is informative, but also impressive. Colleges seek motivated, creative students who take responsibility for their education and learning, and ultimately adding to the diversity of their campuses.

Record Keeping Tip

Use descriptive adjectives and nouns to tell the reader about your student.

Motivated	Intuitive	Peer counselor	Representative	Generous	Leader
Imaginative	Talented	Creative	Musician	Artist	Athlete
Director	Actor	President	Innovative	Articulate	Scholar
Determined	Prepared	Employee	Manager	Organized	Avid
Resourceful	Exceptional	Informed	Proficient	Specialist	Expert
Certified	Licensed	Operator	Knowledgeable	Experienced	

- **The Course**

Think about the course. What were the specific requirements for the course? How was the course taught? Who taught the course? Was it a traditional course or an independent study? Your answers will give an admissions officer a thorough synopsis of your student's education.

Document the specific requirements for the course, explaining how the content was taught, how the student learned the material, and how the student performed in a variety of educational settings. Use measurable and accurate statements. Writing a course description with specific details is valuable for every course, but especially for courses taught without a textbook or workbook.

Record Keeping Tip

Record the educational settings in which the student studies. These should be included in the course descriptions.

Independent study	Work study	Collaboration	Classroom instruction
Laboratory experience	Internship	Job shadowing	Apprenticeship
Field work	Studio	Market research	

Using the educational setting and the expectations of the course, the parent can begin writing the description.

• The student participated on an AAU and USSSA sanctioned, competitive baseball team, developing pitching and fielding skills, while enhancing his knowledge of strategy and play. Requirements included playing games during the fall season, attending mandatory practices, and playing in state competition. In addition, the student volunteered as a coach's assistant for a younger thirteen-year-old team, helping players with conditioning and fielding.

• The student completed two quilting courses through a local sewing studio: Quilting for Beginners and Advanced Quilting.

• The course was deemed complete when the shed passed the final inspection of occupancy.

• Observation, interaction and practical experience with children and their parents was required for this course.

• The student participated in individual group games and activities including ultimate Frisbee, tennis, kickball, volleyball, basketball, golf, soccer, and water sports.

If the content of your student's class included higher level thinking skills, use terminology to describe what took place. Be sure to pack the description with active verbs and educational language, while being honest and concise. A college administrator's natural curiosity about a student educated at home will work in your favor. Satisfy his or her curiosity.

Record Keeping Tip

Use active words when developing objectives or writing course descriptions.

Observe	Rehearse	Apply	Analyze	Demonstrate
Paint	Debate	Summarize	Evaluate	Tabulate
Convert	Illustrate	Communicate	Calculate	Dissect
Consult	Exemplify	Display	Propose	Tutor
Train	Query	Integrate	Translate	Utilize
Assemble	Compose	Pilot	Navigate	Travel
Administrate	Construct	Examine	Prepare	Experiment
Research	Articulate	Formulate	Modify	Correlate
Infer	Model	Invent	Collaborate	Compile
Adapt	Negotiate	Lead	Facilitate	Design
Assess	Measure	Conclude	Critique	Hypothesize
Serve	Challenge	Volunteer	Discuss	Exhibit
Expound	Operate	Lobby	Instruct	Perform

Textbook chapter titles are a gold mine of information and a helpful resource for writing course descriptions. Read the chapter titles. Make a list of the concepts your student studied. Use those concepts to create a synopsis of the class.

If resources were used, specify those in the description. Our students used how-to books and online tutorials, owner's manuals, curriculum guides, professional journals, and magazine subscriptions. I included these materials in course descriptions for classes in which they were used.

We designed several courses for our young adults and hence had to write the descriptions so college admissions would understand the scope and depth of the courses. Our oldest son was considering a business-related career. During our weekly family visits to the library, he faithfully read the current issues of business magazines. In addition, he combed the online catalog for business-related books and spent hours in independent study. We discussed what he was reading and encouraged him to talk with local businessmen. He also job shadowed his grandfather, a small business owner, and had several discussions with his uncle, an officer in a company. The extent and application of his learning was astounding so I created a class to incorporate his studies. During an online search, I noticed a high school offered a one-credit course, Business and Entrepreneurial Principles. Much of the content mirrored my son's work. We renamed the course Business Principles and made additional requirements. At the end of the school year, we wrote the course description.

This course provided an introduction to business-related principles and careers. Communication skills, business ownership, organizational structures, management, leadership skills, human resources, and business ethics were among the topics learned. The student read every issue of *INC.* and *Fast Company*, two of his favorite business magazines. In addition, the student chose to further his studies by reading *Lessons from the Top: The Search for America's Best Business Leaders*, *How to Win Friends and Influence People*, and *Good to Great*. Job shadowing, interviews, and conversations with business owners and financial planners were required.

Lab and practical, hands-on experiences should be included in course descriptions when applicable. Though it is obvious to incorporate labs for science-related courses, hands-on experiences are appropriate for auto mechanics, textiles and fabrics, landscape architecture, web design, or horticulture.

Writing your student's story will be easier if you keep a running list of your student's activities, opportunities, achievements, and awards. The list will help you remember events you might otherwise forget and will be helpful if hours are needed for credit.

- Travel opportunities
- Job titles
- Small business owner
- Inventions and patents
- Visits to art galleries, museums, and music halls
- Theater presentations, operas, musical performances, and band competitions
- Interviews and conversations with government officials, dignitaries, and business leaders
- Job shadowing, internships, apprenticeships and teaching opportunities

- Competitive sports titles and awards or lettering in Varsity sports
- Debate and speech competitions
- Government page positions, mock trial opportunities and teen court participant

When writing course descriptions, be sure to acknowledge student achievements associated with the class. Student achievements are often related to completed courses and add merit to course content. Examples might include membership in a foreign language honor society, featured soloist, keynote speaker, published author, community representative, Eagle Scout, state and national titles or honors, and leadership roles. Include significant details. You can delete unnecessary information later, but it is harder to add details after the fact.

Always list the textbooks and resource materials used to complete the course. If the course was taught by the traditional textbook method, this is easy. Simply open the text and write down the title, author, publisher, and copyright date. For courses you design, note the author, date, publisher, and copyright dates of resources. Students intent on registering with the NCAA Clearinghouse should consider photocopying the title page and the table of contents. Primary source documents, biographies, literature pieces, magazine subscriptions, how-to-manuals, seminars, websites, field guides, anthologies, reference materials, and video series are among the limitless resources available in the home learning environment.

Perhaps you are into the high school journey and have not kept records. It is never too late to start. Better late than not at all. Your efforts to retrace steps may determine whether your student lands a highly-sought-after-job or receives an acceptance letter from a selective college. It is worth your time. Do not be afraid to ask your student to help recall the highlights and specifics of completed courses. If they learned it, they'll remember it.

WHEW! The information has been gathered about the student and the course and now you can write your student's intriguing stories, the course descriptions. Remember, employers and admissions officers are looking for exceptional course content, stand-out character traits and abilities, and extraordinary educational opportunities. Add spark to your course descriptions.

Please Note: Though the goal is to add spark to your student's course descriptions, it must be done with honesty and integrity. Do not attempt to stretch the truth or falsify information.

I have added spark to my course descriptions in three ways, by tweaking traditional classes, by allowing my student to stand out, by making our electives extraordinary.

- **Tweak Traditional Courses**

Tweak traditional courses by highlighting your student's unique abilities, achievements, and activities. For example, American history is a required course for most high school students. However, your student may have had the opportunity to enjoy experiential learning which enhanced his or her learning, perhaps touring Civil War battlefields on the East coast, talking with war veterans at an assisted living, or participating in reenactments. Likewise, a visit to government buildings in Washington, D.C., campaigning for a local politician, job shadowing the city mayor, or participating in teen court would complement the reading of an American government text. Extending learning beyond the standard requirements speaks to your student's character as well as to the quality of education.

Survey of American History
1 high school credit

Text: *United States History: Heritage of Freedom*, Michael R. Lowman, George Thompson, and Kurt Grussendorf, A Beka Book, Pensacola Christian College, 1997

Additional resources: primary source documents

This course provided advanced study of the people and events of the United States from Colonial America to the present. In addition to completing all the activities in the text, the student toured Civil War battlefields in Pennsylvania, Virginia, North Carolina, and South Carolina. Additional reading of the student's choice included *The Boys of Ninety-Eight* (Theodore Roosevelt), *Northern Mists*, *The Lost Discovery*, *Fabric of Freedom: 1763-1800*, *American Conquest*, *Father Ten Boom*, and *Hitler*. A research paper was written in defense of the first American explorers.

Speech I
1 high school credit

Text: *The Art of Interpretation*, Nick Ellidge

This course was an introduction to competitive and public speech. Instruction was given in the ten areas of competitive speech including platform, impromptu, extemporaneous and interpretive. The student participated in training at Master's Conference and competed at National Christian Forensics and Communications Association (NCFCA) State, Regional and National Competitions.

American Sign Language I
1 high school credit

Text: *Signing Naturally* Level I, Cheri Smith, Ella Mae Lentz and Ken Mikos, Dawn Sign Press, 1988

As a result of the student's independent study the year prior, she enrolled in an ASL I class taught by a certified ASL interpreter-educator. The class used *Signing Naturally*, a commonly used high school and college curriculum. The student completed the exercises in the book, interpreted a song and two dramatic presentations, attended a luncheon and communicated with attendees who were hearing impaired, and participated in a field trip given by a hearing-impaired chef at a five-star hotel. The student wrote a research essay about the life of Linda Bove and presented the information to her class. In addition to the classroom setting, the student chose to take an eight-week workshop learning basic interpretation in a church setting. The final session of the class was a silent dinner with deaf parishioners.

Philosophy
1 high school credit

Text: *Understanding the Times*, David Noebel, Summit Ministries, 1995

The student studied theology, philosophy, ethics, psychology, and sociology from various worldview perspectives. Additional reading chosen by the student included *What's So Amazing About Grace?*, *The Green Letters: Principles of Spiritual Growth*, *Proving the Unseen*, *Simply Christian*, and *Why We Are Emergent by Two Guys Who Should Be*.

- **Stand-out Student**

Some students are self-motivated, independent, eager learners. These coveted qualities should be evident in the course descriptions, especially for classes initiated or created by the student. College admissions officers are eager to admit students who enjoy learning and are motivated to complete studies.

Survey of Ancient Literature	**0.5 high school credit**

Student interest led to the development of this course. After detailed research and study of ancient history the student read *Complete Works* by Aristotle, *Confessions* by Augustine, *Orations* by Cicero, *Epic of Gilgamesh*, *Mythology* by Edith Hamilton, *The Iliad* and *The Odyssey* by Homer, *The Death of Socrates* by Plato, *Antigone* by Sophocles and *The Aeneid* by Virgil.

Creative Writing	**0.5 high school credit**

This course allowed the student to use her creativity, research skills and personal experiences to produce and edit an extensive piece of creative literature. The student chose to write a historically-accurate chapter book set in pre-revolutionary Boston, *Memoirs of an Apprentice*, intended for upper elementary school students.

Drawing and Painting I	**1 high school credit**

Resources: *Life-like Heads* by Lance Richin, *How Artists View Homes* by Karen Hosack, *How Artist View Nature* by Karen Hosack, and *Draw 50 Famous Faces* by James J. Ames, *Drawing Animals Amazingly Easy* by Christopher Hart, *The Art of Basic Drawing* by Walter Foster, *Drawing Expressive Portraits* by Paul Leveille, *The Art of the Impressionist* by Janice Anderson, and *I Can Draw in 30 Days* by Mark Kistler

This course was initiated by the student whose independent study focused on the fundamentals, principles and elements of design in drawing and painting, as well as working knowledge of various media. Topics included color, contour and contrast; shading and tinting techniques; still life; portraiture; collage; and perspective. Media included charcoal, drawing pencils, watercolor, acrylics, and oil paints. Studies incorporated famous artists, art history, and art appreciation. In addition, the student displayed her works at two public events and critiqued art exhibited at local art gallery. The student visited and discussed art exhibits at Flagler College, The John and Mable Ringling Museum of Art, The Crummer Museum of Art and Gardens, and The Albin Polasek Museum.

Personal Fitness I	**0.5 high school credit**

Understanding the need for life fitness and good nutrition to maintain health, the student designed this course to develop, to carry out, and to maintain a daily personal fitness routine to build endurance, while eating nutritionally-balanced meals. Her plan included daily activity in one or more of the following: stretching, light weight lifting, biking, walking, swimming, and elliptical workout.

- **Extraordinary Electives**

Electives represent the interests, talents and curiosities of a student. Driver's Education may not turn the heads of the admissions committee but Introduction to Pediatric Medicine, Floral Design, Care and Concerns of the Elderly, or Independent Study: Russian History may intrigue the reader enough to consult a corresponding course description or ask a question in a personal interview. A distinctive course title begs a second look and further inquiry into the student.

Parents often ask about earning elective credit. I answer by helping them think about what the student is already doing. For example, this week I met with a parent and student. The student is involved in a local homeless ministry. She is currently training new volunteers and has recently been asked if she would like to attend counseling sessions between the director and clients. This opportunity would give the student a chance to learn how she might be able to counsel and encourage peers who are homeless. Essentially she is learning how to be a peer counselor. Upon researching electives offered at the local high school, we determined her learning opportunity parallels the objectives of the peer counseling course. Hence, the mother is considering awarding her daughter credit in peer counseling and adding the course to the student transcript.

Introduction to Building Construction   **1 high school credit**
Resources: *How to Build a Shed*

The student completed the requirements of this course in conjunction with earning his Eagle Scout Award. Course work included researching the building of a 8x12 utility shed, designing and drawing the building plans, collaborating with a state-certified general contractor for building code, meeting with city officials, discussing zoning, creating a materials budget, purchasing supplies, coordinating work teams and sub-contractors, and scheduling inspections. The student was actively involved in framing the foundation, pouring the concrete slab, framing, sheathing, roofing, and siding work. The course was deemed complete when the shed passed the final inspection of occupancy.

Floral Design   **0.5 high school credit**

This course introduced the student to the basic elements of floral design. Content included tools, supplies and equipment for floral design; wire and taping technique; care and handling of fresh flowers; flower and foliage identification; design; marketing and pricing; and careers in floral design. The student assisted the designer at a local florist.

Nutrition and Wellness   **0.5 high school credit**

The purpose of this course was to familiarize the student with the relationship between nutrition and wellness by planning meals, developing skills in food preparation, understanding nutritional needs, analyzing the psychological aspects of foods, and exploring food related careers. Instruction was given in budgeting, meal preparation, safe handling of food, appropriate use of small and large kitchen appliances, and the handling and care of kitchen tools and equipment. The student researched and experimented with recipe options for people choosing to eat gluten free, vegan, and raw.

A Reason to Celebrate

My course descriptions were derived in different ways. When sitting down to write a description, the first place I looked for course content information was on the curriculum website. Many sites detail exactly what each of their courses cover. Once I found the information, I paraphrased specifics and then added any extra studies or materials assigned by me. The second place I went for help was homeschool curriculum review sites. A reviewer is usually are pretty clear in their description of a course before giving their review. For math courses I used the table of contents and listed what was covered in the course.

Choosing Course Titles

Course titles make a difference in the admissions process, especially if they are unique. In fact, they can often be the first item to pop off the page, whether on a transcript or on a course description document. If indeed the course titles are to jump off the page, they need to intrigue, to demand a second read, to tell the reader there is more to uncover.

Parents tell me they struggle with "what to call it", meaning they have recorded content of a course, perhaps even wrote a description, but writer's block settles in when they begin to think about titles. I encourage them to do what I have done: research.

When I get stumped, I read online curriculum guides or search course titles in the corresponding subject area. College offerings have also been helpful, especially when our student has studied a topic not generally offered in high school. Reading titles, even course syllabi, inspire my creativity as I endeavor to communicate the accolades of my high schooler. I want course titles to capture the attention of the reader and to offer a snapshot of the strengths, interests and talents of my student. If my efforts garner an offer from the student's top choice college, the time spent is well worth the sacrifice.

A Reason to Celebrate

As a parent of a home education student with highly selective, competitive universities on the top college choice list, I found those schools expected our courses to be as rigorous as Honors, International Baccalaureate (IB), and Advanced Placement (AP) courses. Interestingly, one school prohibited me from labeling any home courses as honors — it was insinuated I did not know what an honors course would entail. I was in a dilemma. How would I prove our courses were rigorous — I researched the content of honors, IB, and AP courses and aimed above those requirements — if I could not title the courses according to their rigor? Granted, my student could have taken honors or AP courses online and scored well on corresponding exams, but he did not enjoy online classes. He also did not want to dual enroll. To prove my son had successfully completed demanding course work required by highly competitive universities, I submitted course descriptions for all his courses as well as a cumulative reading list from his four-year trek. He was accepted and offered Presidential scholarships at both schools, each scholarship worth more than $32,000 per year. I had to go the extra mile to prove my son had received a competitive education. My research and extra work on documents was worth the time.

(SAMPLE FORMAT)

Course Descriptions for
(Student Name)

English I/ American Literature   1 high school credit
Text: *Literature of American People: Classics for Christians*, Jan Anderson and Laurel Hicks, ABeka Books, Pensacola Christian College, 1996
Write for College, Patrick Sebranek, Verne Meyer and Dave Kemper, Write Source, Great Source Education Group, Houghton Mifflin, 1997
Additional literature pieces: *To Kill a Mockingbird, The Red Badge of Courage, The Hiding Place, Lord of the Flies, The Adventures of Huckleberry Finn, The Old Man and the Sea,* and *The Sun Also Rises.*

The goal of this course was to provide an avenue for the development and application of English language arts through enriching experiences in literature, writing, speaking and listening, while expecting academic excellence. Instruction was given in applying the writing process to creative and formal writing; public speaking; and critical analysis of major American literary genres, including nonfiction, biography, poetry, the short story, drama and the novel. Writing assignments included multi-paragraph essays, a documented research paper, book reviews, persuasive essays, narratives, and expository writing.

Creative Writing   0.5 high school credit

This course allowed the student to use his creativity, his research skills and his personal experiences to produce and edit an extensive piece of creative literature. The student chose to compose a historically accurate chapter book, set in pre-revolutionary Boston, entitled *Memoirs of an Apprentice*, intended for an audience of upper elementary school students.

Algebra II   1 high school credit
Text: *Algebra II: An Incremental Development*, John H. Saxon Jr., Saxon Publishers, Second Edition, 1992

Student completed lessons in the required text providing the foundation for more advanced mathematical courses. Topics of study included equation of the line, radicals, polynomials, power of sums, linear intercepts, quadratic equations, proofs, slope formulas, linear inequalities, parabolas, and logarithms.

Consumer and Business Mathematics   1 high school credit
Text: *Consumer Mathematics, Abeka Book, Pennsacola Christian College, 1998*

The student initiated this class by her interest in personal finance. She actively recorded her income and expenses from her small business, organized and registered receipts, filed federal income and state sales tax, started a saving and tithing budget, and initiated couponing and comparison savings for the family budget. Other topics related to math and life skills included the operating and maintenance cost to buying a car; figuring hourly wages, business expenses, and self-employment taxes; itemizing expenses; renting and mortgage rates; homeowner's insurance; unit pricing for foods; food labeling and nutrition as related to budgeting; developing a clothing budget comparing thrift and retail purchasing; opening and maintaining a checking account; purchasing insurance and stocks; and credit.

| Student Name | Birth Date | Course Description | Page # |

Chemistry
1 high school credit

Text: *Exploring Creation with Chemistry*, Dr. Jay L. Wile, Apologia Educational Ministries, Inc., Second Edition, 2003.

A lab oriented course, the student completed all reading, study questions, and module tests in the text independently and participated in a weekly lab/lecture class, taught by a high school chemistry instructor, where he worked collectively with his peers to complete lab experiences.

Survey of Botony, Horticulture and Landscaping
1 high school credit

Resource: *Square Foot Gardening: A New Way to Garden in Less Space with Less Work* by Mel Bartholomew

This course was an independent study motivated by the student's interest to design a functional, edible landscape. Her studies included chemical and natural pest control; soil composition and composting; differences between annuals, biennials, and perennial; growing conditions; nutrients needed for plant growth; use of fertilizer; hydroponics; flower, herb, vegetable, and landscape design and care; plant and seed propagation and harvesting; cuts and transplants; greenhousing; home and business cultivation; building climbing trellis; floral design and arranging; dissecting and identifying parts of a flower; and designing a butterfly garden. The student made two visits—one including a tour of the facility—to ECHO farms training facility, and several visits nursery and garden shops. The student utilized You Tube tutorials for planting, care, and harvesting techniques.

Human Anatomy and Physiology
1 high school credit

Text: *The Human Body: Fearfully and Wonderfully Made*, Dr. Jay Wile, Apologia Educational Ministries, 2001
The Human Body Coloring Book, DK

A lab oriented, in-depth course covering the eleven organ systems of the human body, the student completed all reading and related study questions in the text independently. Online video lessons supplemented the textbook. The student utilized You Tube and Khan Academy tutorials to enhance her study. Multiple visits to the Chiropractor afforded the student to listen to the doctor talk about lower extremity muscles and how exercise affects their function. The student also asked the doctor about his professional training and his recommendations for students considering this field.

American History
1 high school credit

Text: *United States History: Heritage of Freedom*, Michael R. Lowman, George Thompson, and Kurt Grussendorf, A Beka Book, Pensacola Christian College, 1997

Additional resources: primary source documents

The goal of this course was to provide advanced study of the people and events responsible for the United States becoming a world leader and economic giant, as well as the process and problems that resulted. Study began with the Post-Reconstruction period and continued, with an emphasis on Post World War II to the present. Additional reading of the student's choice included *The Boys of Ninety-Eight* (Theodore Roosevelt), *Northern Mists*, *The Lost Discovery*, *Fabric of Freedom: 1763-1800*, *American Conquest*, *Father Ten Boom*, and *Hitler*. A research paper was written in defense of the first American explorers.

Spanish I
1 high school credit

The student completed this one year high school course through the Florida Virtual School, an on-line accredited Florida public school.

Student Name	Birth Date	Course Description	Page #

Drawing and Painting I

1 high school credit

This full-year course, taken with homeschool students, was instructed by a watercolorist and focused on the fundamentals, principles and elements of design in drawing and painting, as well as working knowledge of various media. Color, contour and contrast; shading and tinting techniques; still life; portraiture; collage; perspective; and calligraphy were studied using charcoal, drawing pencils, felt tip pen, calligraphy pens, watercolor and acrylics. Studies incorporated famous artists, art history, and art appreciation. Student mounted and displayed works at two public events, critiqued exhibited art at local art gallery and presented researched material on an artist to his peers.

Introduction to Building Construction

1 high school credit

Resources: *How to Build a Shed*

The student completed the requirements of this course in conjunction with earning his Eagle Scout Award. Coursework included researching the building of a 8x12 utility shed, designing and drawing the building plans, collaborating with a state-certified general contractor in regards to building code, having blueprints made, meeting with city officials, discussing zoning, relocating landscaping, creating a materials budget, purchasing supplies, coordinating work teams, coordinating sub-contractors, and scheduling inspections. The student was actively involved in framing the foundation, pouring the concrete slab, framing, sheathing, roofing, and siding work. The course was deemed complete when the shed passed the final inspection of occupancy.

Nutrition and Wellness

0.5 high school credit

The purpose of this course was to familiarize the student with the relationship between nutrition and wellness by planning meals, developing skills in food preparation, understanding nutritional needs, analyzing the psychological aspects of foods, and exploring food related careers. Instruction was given in budgeting, meal preparation, safe handling of food, appropriate use of small and large kitchen appliances, and the handling and care of kitchen tools and equipment.

Personal Fitness II

0.5 high school credit

Emphasizing the need for life fitness and good nutrition to maintain health, this course built on the fundamentals learned in Personal Fitness I, requiring the student to develop, to participate in, and to maintain a daily fitness routine, while eating nutritionally balanced meals and building endurance. Daily activity in one or more of the following: stretching, running, biking, walking, swimming and light weight training were included in his plan. The course included 12 visits with a personal trainer.

Team Sports I

0.5 high school credit

Reading: *The Mental Game of Baseball*, H.A Dorfman and Karl Kuehl
Between the Lines, Orel Hershiser

Student participated on an AAU and USSSA sanctioned, competitive baseball team developing pitching and fielding skills, while enhancing his knowledge of strategies of sports play. Requirements included playing in over 75 games in the spring season, attending two weekly practices and traveling with the team to in-state games including Gainesville and Lakeland. The student also participated in a weekend trip to play top Atlanta teams, a trip to the Road to Omaha in Nebraska, AAU State Championships and AAU National Championships.

Student Name	Birth Date	Course Description	Page #

Sample Course Titles

English
English I-IV
English I/ Survey of American Literature
English I/Survey of Early American Literature
English Language and Composition
English II/Survey of British Literature
English III/Survey of World Literature
English IV/Survey of Ancient World Literature
English IV/Survey of Contemporary Literature
College English
Introduction to Children's Literature
Shakespearean Theater
Greco-Roman Theater
Short Stories
Poetry and Short Stories
Creative Writing
Writing for Print and Publication
Journalism
Yearbook
Screenwriting
Desktop Publishing

Communications
Speech
Beginning Speech
Intermediate Speech
Competitive Speech
Speech Technique: Impromptu
Speech Technique:Expository
Debate
Policy Debate
Media Productions
Mass Media

Mathematics
Business Math
Consumer Math
Integrated Math
Algebra I
Algebra II
College Algebra
Geometry
Pre-Calculus
Calculus
Advanced Mathematics
Probability & Statistics
Analytical Geometry
Trigonometry
Statistics
Business Mathematics
Consumer Mathematics

Social Sciences
Early American History
Modern American History
American Government
Government and Politics
Comparative Government
Introduction to Law
Constitutional Law
Independent Study: Foreign Policy
Independent Study: Criminal Justice
Mock Trial
Consumer Economics
Economics
Macroeconomics
Ancient World History
Modern World History
History of Western Civilizations
Ancient Civilizations
Independent Study: Middle East History
Independent Study: Korean War
World History
European History
Medieval History
World Geography
Psychology
Introduction to Social Work
Introduction to Sociology
Introduction to Anthropology
Child and Adolescent Psychology
Philosophy
World Religions

Sciences
Environmental Science
Animal and Agricultural Sciences
Botany
Biology
Marine Biology
Marine Science
Astronomy
Introduction to Aerospace Science
Chemistry
Physics
Advanced Physics

Anatomy and Physiology
Independent Study: Forensics

Foreign Language
Latin I-IV
Spanish I-IV
French I-IV
German I-IV
Italian I-IV
Russian I-IV
Japanese I-IV
Chinese I-IV
Ancient Languages
Latin I-IV
Greek I-IV
Hebrew I-IV
American Sign Language (not always considered
foreign language)

Performing Arts/Fine Arts
Introduction to Drama
Introduction to Theater
Musical Theater
Art History
Choreography
Dance Technique I
Competitive Dance
Introduction to Ballroom Dance
Stagecraft
Set Design
Theater Production
Art Appreciation
Two Dimensional Art
Sculpture
Ceramics
Drawing and Painting
Cartooning and Caricature
Printmaking
Pottery
Photography

Music
Band
Orchestra
Symphonic Band
Wind Ensemble
Jazz Ensemble
Keyboard
Piano
Music Theory

Music History
Music Appreciation

Physical Education
Personal Fitness
Physical Education
Aerobics
Tennis
Golf
Volleyball
Competitive Swimming
Water Polo
Lifesaving
Advanced Lifesaving
Team Sports
Recreational Sports
Beginning Weights
Weight Training
Sports Physiology
Sports Medicine
Sports Rehabilitation

Business Education
Accounting
Marketing
Personal Finance
Banking and Finance
Business Principles
Independent Study: Business Law
Entrepreneurial Principles
Managerial Principles
Foundational Principles of Small Business
Keyboarding
Word Processing
Graphic Design
Business Technology
Web Design

Computer Science
Computer Programming
Computer Science
Introduction to Computer Systems
Introduction to Computer Technology
Computer Construction and Repair

Vocational Trade
Cosmetology
Cabinet Making
Masonry

Carpentry
Trim and Finish Carpentry
Landscaping
Landscape Architecture
Building Design and Architecture
Horticulture
Engineering
Drafting
Technical Drawing
Plumbing
Welding
Auto Mechanics
Diesel Mechanics
Small Engine Repair
Electronics and Circuitry

Home Economics

Interior Design
Floral Design
Principles in Food Preparation
Principles in Food Preparation: Pastries
Principles in Food Preparation: Desserts
Principles in Food Preparation: Main Courses
Principles in Food Preparation: Appetizers
Cake Decorating
Fashion Design
Clothing Construction and Textiles
Introduction to Machine Sewing
Quilting and Appliqué
Needlecraft and Hand Sewing
Child and Adolescent Development
Nutrition
Driver's Education
Home and Automotive Repair
First Aid and CPR

Electives

Horsemanship
Introduction of Horse Anatomy and Care
Introduction to Veterinary Science
Introduction to Early Childhood Education
Biblical Studies: Old Testament
Biblical Studies: New Testament
Theology
Independent Study: Youth Ministry
Independent Study: Church History

A transcript is a written summary—a visual representation—of your student's high school experience. This paper will represent your student, the student's educational experience, and your homeschool. The transcript must be concise and presented in a clear, easy-to-read format. Make it look professional. Presentation is everything if you want administrators to take your student's home education seriously.

Accurate record keeping is essential to transcript development. Organizing important documents—course information and test scores specifically—in one place helped me to create a transcript template. As my student completed a course, I added course titles, grades, and credits. I computed the grade point average when necessary.

On the admission journeys with our high schoolers, I have learned colleges look for specific information on transcripts and application documents. Including the needed, and often required, information when applying gives college personnel time to learn about the student instead of taking time to make additional inquiries.

Record Keeping Tip

What information should I include on my student's transcript?

Accurate record keeping is key to transcript development. Save documents which will help you include needed information.

- Student's name, address, and phone number
- Student's birth date and gender
- Student's social security number
- Parent's names and address
- Name and address of the school
- Issue date of the transcript
- Graduation date (or anticipated graduation date)
- Courses completed or currently enrolled by year (be sure to use concise titles)
- Grade assigned to each course (most colleges use alphabetic grading scale: A, B, C, D or F)
- A grading scale (in percentages) used to assign grades to the student
- Denote courses not taken at home: online, community college, four-year university
- Credit hours earned
- GPA and cumulative GPA
- Test scores (PSAT, SAT, ACT, CLEP and DANTES, if appropriate)
- Parent signature and date

When I began my first high school journey I was advised by another parent to list my courses by content area rather than academic year. In other words, all English courses were to be listed together instead of one English each academic year. Though the parent's reasoning made sense to me at the time, every college my son applied to wanted courses listed in the academic year which they were taken. Therefore, I had to rework my transcript template before applying. Essentially, I had to redo the transcript. Due to that experience, I now check online to learn if the college has a transcript preference sample or ask the home education admission specialist which format is preferred.

Course titles, as discussed on page 83 should reflect the content of the class and be self-explanatory. When placing course titles in the document, be sure to use the same order for every year. For example, English listed first with math second, natural science third, social science fourth, followed by electives. Each successive year, courses should be listed in that same order. The visual presentation and course titles should give the readers an accurate picture of what the student will bring to the campus community.

Test scores are usually included on the transcript. Only SAT, ACT, SAT Subject Test, AP, CLEP and DANTE scores should be recorded. Colleges are not interested in nationally-normed achievement test scores.

I used the same general transcript template for all three of my high school students. With the template complete I simply added pertinent information and repositioned items for visual appeal. This was much easier than starting from scratch every time we had a high school student.

A Reason to Celebrate

Having covered the typical literary works in both British and American literature, my high school daughter's zeal for reading led me to suggest a classic Agatha Christie mystery novel. She picked up And Then There Were None. *Subsequently, a magazine article highlighting a contemporary of Christie's, author Dorothy Sayers, led my daughter to read several of Sayer's Lord Peter Wimsey detective novels. The enthusiasm for this genre grew. My daughter's interest in G.K. Chesterton's theological writings reacquainted her with his Father Brown mystery series. Her passion for British mystery continued to grow and I became intrigued. Together, she and I became sleuths, searching for more. In our search, we discovered these early twentieth century British authors—Christie, Sayers, and Chesterton—were among the founding members of The Detection Club, a society of mystery fiction writers still in existence today.*

When we sketched out our daughter's four-year plan I had no inclination to create a British Mystery Literature course. However, along her learning journey, as the interest in British mystery grew from her reading, I felt my daughter's hours of learning (and enjoyment!) merited a half-credit course. As I finalized her transcript, I added British Mystery Literature as an elective class.

Grading

Parents often ask how to assign grades to their student's work. If the student is completing a question-answer assignment—like math problems or a chapter review in history—or taking a multiple choice test, the grading is easy. The answer is either right or wrong. This type of grade is objective. If the grading is more subjective—based on an opinion—as when grading an essay, grade assignment becomes a bit more difficult. For subjective assignments, a rubric (a chart which states specifically how the assignment will be graded, what will be expected, and what point value will be assigned to the submission) is the best option for grading. Rubrics can be found online.

There have been some courses for which there were no right or wrong answers, no percentages, and no rubrics. For example, when my son was building the shed for his Eagle Scout project, the final grade was based on whether or not he received a certificate of occupancy from the city as well as his character and work ethic as he progressed through the project. I created a document, a list of adjectives, by which I would "grade" those courses. This list of adjectives helped me grade the course, but also helped the student know the expectations. It would have also been easy to explain to college personnel or employers should they have inquired about the grading of such courses.

A- Exceptional, Excellent, Extraordinary, Superior
B- Commendable, Good, Praiseworthy, Above Average, Creditable
C- Adequate, Ordinary, Average, Usual
D- Fair, Minimal, Insufficient, Lacking
F - Unacceptable, Incomplete, Failure, Poor

Calculating Grade Point Averages

Points are assigned to the letter grades your student earns. These points calculate the grade point average. Generally, more difficult classes—honors, AP and dual enrollment—earn more points, raising the grade point average to reflect the student's rigorous schedule. Florida Bright Futures adds one-half point for weighted courses. In other words, a letter grade of A in an unweighted full-year, one-credit course would be assigned a 4.0. A letter grade of A in a weighted full-year, one-credit course would be assigned a 4.5. Similarly, a letter grade of B in an unweighted full-year, one-credit course would be assigned a 3.0. A letter grade of B in a weighted full-year, one-credit course would be assigned a 3.5.

In our experiences, we found that not all colleges weigh classes by the same means. Some colleges post their weighting criteria on their sites. Others do not. Be sure to check before calling to inquire.

After speaking to many admissions offices, each with different standards and many telling me "they would recalculate the GPA anyway", I decided to calculate our student's GPA on a 4.0 scale. I made sure to note on the student's transcript that the GPA was based on an **unweighted** 4.0 scale. In addition, one university told me they recalculated home school transcripts because they had no standard means by which to determine if a homeschool course was honors worthy. That college would only accept honors credit from an accredited school. Knowing that information, I submitted my high schooler's course descriptions so the college admissions personnel could indeed verify my son had done Honors level or above work. That college, at first skeptical of my grading and my son's course content, actually invited him to be a part of their honors college. My extra work paid dividends in the end.

As you navigate your student's college admission, be sure to ask officials what grade point they assign to grades for honors, AP, and dual enrollment classes, should you decide to weight the classes.

To calculate the GPA

- Assign a numerical value to the grades earned. For standard level classes, it is assumed that A=4, B=3, C=2, D=1, and F=0. This is called a four-point scale. Honors and AP classes are generally weighted on a five-point scale, though this scale is not standard and may vary. Research which scale your state Department of Education uses and consider using their scale as your guide, especially if your student will be attending a state university and competing for admission with other students from your state.

	Grade	Credit	GP	Ex
English I	A	1.0	4	4.0
Algebra	B	1.0	3	3.0
Biology	B	1.0	3	3.0
Am. History	A	1.0	4	4.0
Personal Fit.	B	0.5	3	1.5
Driver's Ed.	A	0.5	4	2.0
Totals		**5.0**	**3.5**	**17.5**

- Write the number of credits earned for each course.

- Multiply the grade point by the credit earned. This is called the extension.

- Total the credits and the extensions.

- Divide the total extensions by the total credits to obtain the GPA.

When calculating a cumulative GPA, count every course for every year and then figure the GPA as above. Do not sum total all GPA's from all four years and then average. This will be incorrect.

A Reason to Celebrate

Immense enjoyment of French I and French II, taken through Florida Virtual School, led my high school senior to decide she would add a French minor to her future college degree. Fueling my daughter's interest in and knowledge of all things French, it occurred to me that a French history course would be a perfect half-credit elective for her final year of home education. I searched the Internet to see if anyone "out there" was teaching a similar course on a high school or college level. My initial search led to investigating French history texts. I found two highly esteemed, well-written, visually-rich resources and purchased both online. My daughter and I began reading and learning, then seeking further resources as our interests were piqued. I knew I needed to find a means by which to evaluate my daughter's understanding of the material in order to declare a grade on her transcript. I created chapter tests with a variety of multiple choice, true-false, fill-in-the-blank, and longer reflection questions. She indeed did enjoy the class, a perfect way to continue her French learning quest and end our senior year together. Our study of French history — titled History of France — was fascinating and a wonderful shared experience!

Student Name:	S.S#:		School: Home School
Address:			Date of Issue: May 15, 2008
Phone:	Date of Birth:		Date of Anticipated Graduation: May 20, 2008
Parents:			Status: Senior Total Credits: 33.5

Student Academic Record

Academic Year: 2003-2004 (Grade 8: high school level courses)

Course	Grade	Credit
Algebra I	A	1.0
Biology I (with lab)	A	1.0
Drawing and Painting I	A	0.5
Total Credits		2.5
GPA	4.0	

Summer 2004 (Grade 9)

Course	Grade	Credit
English I/American Literature	A	1.0
American History	A	1.0
Personal Fitness I	A	0.5
Life Management Skills	A	0.5
Team Sports I	A	0.5
Total Credits		3.5
GPA	4.0	

Academic Year: 2004-2005 (Grade 9)

Course	Grade	Credit
Algebra II	A	1.0
English II/World Literature	A	1.0
Modern World History	A	1.0
Chemistry (with lab)	A	1.0
Economics	A	0.5
Drama I	A	1.0
Yearbook	A	0.5
Team Sports II	A	0.5
Beginning Weights	A	0.5
Total Credits		7.0
GPA	4.0	
Cum GPA	4.0	

Summer: 2005 (Grade 10)

Course	Grade	Credit
Intermediate Weights	A	0.5
Creative Writing	A	0.5
Total Credits		1.0
GPA	4.0	

Academic Year: 2005-2006 (Grade 10)

Course	Grade	Credit
Geometry	B	1.0
English III/Ancient Literature	A	1.0
Ancient World History	A	1.0
Physics	B	1.0
Driver's Education	A	0.5
Recreational Sports	A	0.5
Personal Fitness II	A	0.5
Total Credits		5.5
GPA	3.64	
Cum GPA	3.90	

Summer: 2006 (Grade 11)

Course	Grade	Credit
Advanced Weights	A	0.5
Nutrition	A	0.5
Total Credits		1.0
GPA	4.0	

Academic Year: 2006-2007 (Grade 11)

Course	Grade	Credit
Analytic Geometry	B	0.5
Trigonometry	B	0.5
English IV/British Literature	A	1.0
American Government	A	0.5
Anatomy & Physiology (with lab)	A	1.0
Spanish I	A	1.0*
Business Systems & Technology	A	1.0*
SAT Prep	A	0.5*
Team Sports III	A	0.5
Total Credits		6.5
GPA	3.80	

Summer: 2007 (Grade 12)

Course	Grade	Credit
Introduction to Computer Gaming	A	0.5
Total Credits		0.5
GPA	4.0	

Academic Year: 2007-2008 (Grade 12)

Course	Grade	Credit
English V/Contemporary Literature	A	1.0
Philosophy	B	1.0
Spanish II	A	1.0*
Computer Programming I	A	1.0*
Child and Adolescent Development	B	1.0
Business Principles	B	1.0
Total Credits		6.0
GPA	3.5	
Cum GPA	3.82	

* Denotes courses taken on-line through the Florida Virtual School
Florida Grading Scale: 90-100 A   80-89 B   70-79 C

Mathematics 4.0	English 4.5	Social Sciences 5.0
Natural Sciences 4.0	Foreign Language 2.0	Fine Arts 1.5
Business Education 3.0	Physical Education 5.0	Other 3.5
		Total Credits

SAT 12/06 Critical Reading ___ Math ___ Writing Skills___
ACT 06/07 Composite Score ____

Administrator   Contact Phone Number   Date

OFFICIAL HIGH SCHOOL TRANSCRIPT

Student Name:	Anna Susan Smith
Address:	123 Main St., Anytown, FL 32765
Soc. Security #:	000-00-0000
Phone:	(407) 555-1212
Birth Date:	01/01/1996
Gender:	Female
Parents:	Mom & Dad Smith *(same address & phone)*

School Name:	Our Homeschool
Date of Issue:	05/31/2013
Graduation Date:	05/31/2015
Current Status:	Senior
Credits Earned:	24
Cumulative GPA:	4.0 weighted unweighted
Class Rank:	1 of 1

Grade 9 – Academic Year: 2011-12	1st Sem	2nd Sem	Credits
English I/Survey of American Literature	A	A	1.0
Algebra I	A	A	1.0
Biology FLVS	A	A	1.0
American History	A	A	1.0
Creative Photography FLVS	A	A	1.0
Drawing and Painting I	A	A	1.0
Cello Performance	A	--	0.5
Music Theory	--	A	0.5
Cumulative GPA: 4.0	Yearly GPA:4.0		Yearly Credits: 7.0

Grade 10 – Academic Year: 2012-13	1st Sem	2nd Sem	Credits
English II/Survey of World Literature	A	A	1.0
Geometry	A	A	1.0
Chemistry	A	A	1.0
World History	A	A	1.0
Consumer and Business Math	A	A	1.0
Sculpture	A	--	0.5
Orchestra	A	A	0.5
Music Theory II	--	A	0.5
Personal Fitness & Nutrition	--	A	0.5
Driver Education/Traffic Safety FLVS	A	--	0.5
Cumulative GPA: 4.0	Yearly GPA: 4.0		Yearly Credits: 7.5

Grade 11 – Academic Year: 2013-14	1st Sem	2nd Sem	Credits
College English I SSC	A	--	1.0
College English II SSC	--	A	1.0
Algebra II	--	A	1.0
Physics	A	A	1.0
Western Civilization I	A	A	1.0
Spanish I	A	A	1.0
Orchestra	A	A	0.5
First Aid and Emergency Preparedness	--	A	0.5
Cumulative GPA: 4.0	Yearly GPA:4.0		Yearly Credits: 7.0

Grade 12 – Academic Year: 2014-15	1st Sem	2nd Sem	Credits
Speech and Debate	A	A	1.0
College Algebra SSC	A	A	1.0
Introduction to Biology SSC	A	A	1.0
American Government	--	A	0.5
Economics	A	--	0.5
Child and Adolescent Development	A	A	1.0
Sociology	A	A	1.0
Spanish II	A	A	1.0
AP Studio Art 2-D	--	A	0.5
Cumulative GPA:4.0	Yearly GPA:4.0		Yearly Credits:7.5

Standardized Test Scores

Test	PSAT	PSAT	SAT
DateTaken	10/12	10/13	4/14
Crit. Reading	80	80	
Math	80	80	
Writing	80	80	

Test	ACT	ACT	ACT
DateTaken	2/12	3/13	5/13
Composite	**36**	**36**	
English	36	36	
Math	36	36	
Reading	36	36	
Science	36	36	
Eng./Writing	36	36	

AP & CLEP Tests

Date Taken	Course Title	Score
07/2013	Western Civilization I	
05/2014	AP Studio Art: 2-D Art	

Total Credits Earned

	7-9th	10th	11th	12th
English	1.0	1.0	2.0	--
Math	2.0	2.0	1.0	1.0
Science	2.0	1.0	1.0	1.0
Social Studies	1.0	1.0	1.0	2.0
Foreign Language	--	--	1.0	1.0
Fine/Perform. Arts	3.0	1.5	0.5	0.5
PE/Personal Fit.	--	0.5	--	
Electives	--	0.5	0.5	2.0
Total	9.0	7.5	7.0	7.5

FLVS Course taken online through Florida Virtual School
SSC Course take at Seminole State College

Key to Grading

A	90-100
B	80-89
C	70-79
D	60-69
F	Below 60

I, Beau Smith, do hereby certify and affirm that this is the official high school transcript of Anna Susan Smith.

_____
Beau Smith

_____
Date

Supporting and supplemental documents, created from cumulative records kept during the high school years, complement the high school transcript and are submitted as part of a college admission packet. Begin keeping records as soon as your student takes high school level courses. Be honest. Do not pre-date materials. Officials will verify records, especially community service hours required for scholarships. Lack of integrity could adversely affect your student's admission.

We keep our cumulative high school records in a three-ring binder divided by section: a reading list, co-curricular activities, community service/volunteer hours, work experience, letters of recommendation, writing samples, certificates, awards and achievements, test results, medical records, college admission applications/information, and financial aid information.

Reading List

Our students keep a cumulative reading list, recording title and author, of every high school (or higher) level book read. Additional information about reading lists is found on page 100. High school literature lists begin on page 102 and a sample student reading list document is printed on page 109.

Co-curricular Activities

Employers and colleges want to know students spent their free time. Did your student play sports, sing in choir, participate in scouts, tutor younger students, train service animals, or compete in chess tournaments? Make note. These are the types of activities which intrigue college officials and help them get to know the student's interests and activities outside of academics. Recording the date and the hours per day the student participated in the activity will be helpful when it comes time to complete college applications. In addition, make note of any leadership titles your student earned. Examples might include first chair cellist, team captain, choir president, youth leader, or volunteer of the year. This information will also be helpful when writing the first resume. The co-curricular log we submitted for our student can be found on page 111.

Community Service Hours & Volunteer Opportunities

Document hours as your student serves. If your student cleans kennels for a local animal shelter, write the supervisor and request documentation of the hours on the organization's letterhead. Include the name, address and phone number of the organization, the name of the supervisor, the service dates, and the total number of hours served. If you desire community service information in a specific format, pre-write the letter and email it, asking the supervisor to print it on company letterhead. You will receive the letter in a timely manner and save the supervisor time. Put the letter in a plastic sleeve and file in the student's records. Our sample letters can be found on page 112.

Work Experience

A record of the student's work experience will be needed for resumes and college applications. We created a spreadsheet, recording work locations, contact addresses and phone numbers, supervisor's names, employment start and end dates, and job description and titles given to the student. All of this information easily transcribed to official documents we needed.

Letters of Recommendation

I have been told letters of recommendation are the second most important documents in a student's admission packet. Why? College admission personnel value—hence require—third party perspectives for applicants. In fact, these letters can often tip the scale when committees are contemplating offering admission to applicants with similar grade point averages and test scores. It is essential that the letters speak to the qualities and achievements of the student as well as how that student will impact the campus community. The more specific the content as related to the campus of application, the better.

Knowing the importance of this document, we choose people who know our high schoolers well and can address their strengths. As our students participate in activities which require mature decisions, reliable work habits, noteworthy character, or courageous leadership, we inquire about the possibility of the supervisor writing a letter of recommendation highlighting these traits. It has been helpful for us to be mindful that universities most often ask for letters of recommendation from pastors, teachers, and employers. We generally collected most of our recommendations during the junior and senior years. However, there have been several situations when we needed a letter from someone who worked with the student during the senior year or a letter in a sealed envelope. We complied with these requests individually. When the letters begin arriving at our home, we place them in plastic sleeves. Records are now being uploaded digitally and will likely take the place of sealed envelope submissions. Specific details for letters of recommendation can be found on page 114 and sample letters are included on page 116.

A Reason to Celebrate

Cheryl's wise counsel to ask for letters of recommendation throughout my daughter's high school years — and not wait until crunch time — allowed us to obtain letters from a variety of sources highlighting my daughter's wide array of interests and abilities. The recommendations offered insight to her leadership responsibilities with church youth, her trustworthiness and dependability in nannying and caregiving positions, her self-directed diligence in a virtual class, and her faithful, patient efforts in community service. The letters we received went into our cumulative high school records notebook for safekeeping until such time as they were needed for applications. From our experiences with letters of recommendation, we learned to ask the person writing the reference to provide two or more personally signed original copies of their letter should we need them for multiple uses.

Writing Samples

Students are often asked to submit essays with college applications. Essay topics and requirements vary from college to college. We found applications and sample essay topics online and got to the business of practicing. Our student's prior writing assignments and experiential opportunities provided good starting points for the essays. By saving writing samples we had a head start on this part of the admission process.

A Reason to Celebrate

I took Cheryl's encouragement to create a cumulative high school records notebook as soon as my daughter began taking high school level courses. Having a single place for hard copies of key documents from virtual high school grade reports to a running chronological reading list and letters of recommendation to immunization records, has saved me time and stress when such items were needed.

Certificates, Awards and Achievements

National Debate Team. Academic Merit. Player of the Year. When certificate awards were bestowed on our students, we protected them with plastic sleeves and filed them in the cumulative folder. These accolades were requested on applications, referred to for scholarships, and used as resources for essays.

Test Results

Test results are now available online. We print the scores, placing copies in the student's cumulative folder. As you receive test scores, file them immediately—yes, voice of experience from a mom who lost the scores and the password to retrieve them! As soon as scores become available, I take time to update the testing section of the student's transcript.

College Admission Applications and Information

As our students express interest in a college, we begin collecting admissions information. We bookmark freshman admission requirements, home education addendums, admission deadlines, and contact emails and phone numbers. As we contact colleges, we note the date of the contact, the person to whom we spoke, his or her phone number and extension, the reason we called, and a brief description of the outcome. This was especially helpful when one of our students turned eighteen during the senior year of high school and administrators would no longer speak to me. With a record of contacts my student and I could both be kept up-to-date in regards to the admission process.

Medical Records

Colleges require a current immunization record and a physical form for college admission. When our students enter high school, I keep up-to-date medical records in their cumulative folder.

Inquire about health policies at the student's top colleges of choice.

☐ Financial Aid Information

This has been a vital section for us to maintain through out the college years as we have referred to it every year since our student has graduated from high school. The information is as important for initial eligibility as it is for renewal. Deadlines, phone numbers, scholarship award letters, financial aid offers, pin numbers, and passwords are just a sampling of records we keep in this section.

Though this list of records may seem daunting, documents come in slowly over a period of four years. With preparation, it is possible to keep accurate records helpful for employment and college admittance. If the documents are filed when received, they will be safe and sound until needed. I cannot count the number of times I have referred to a piece of important information in a student's folder. In the long run, our folders save us time, energy, anxiety, and frustration.

Parents ask how long the cumulative folder should be kept. We add to the folder throughout the student's college career as financial aid materials, medical records, scholarship applications, and other documents change. After college graduation, it is our student's responsibility to decide how long the information is needed based on employment or graduate school. Some parents have kept their students' folders for ten years after high school graduation. Until the young adult is employed permanently with no chance of continuing education or military service, the folder may be needed. A friend of mine recently experienced how important the folder is when, after several years in the military, the young adult applied to the local university. The high school transcript was needed for admission. The cumulative folder has helped many parents navigate employment, postsecondary education and beyond.

A Reason to Celebrate

I got a three-ring binder when my son started 9th grade so I could document and save all of his important high school records in one place. (I have since shared this tip with other moms, including those with teens in public high school.) I divided the notebook into the sections Cheryl suggested to ensure nothing would fall through the cracks. In 9th grade, I only had a few things in my son's binder, but by the time he finished 10th grade and needed to submit a transcript to a college to be accepted as a dual-enrolled student, I was so grateful we had everything in place in his binder. Now that he is in 12th grade, his binder is brimming with recommendation letters, awards, community service work, extracurricular activities, reading lists, and more, all organized neatly and easy to find. Since I am helping him apply for many college scholarships right now, I can honestly say that this binder has saved my sanity and taken some of the stress out of all the paperwork involved in this process.

Read the book. Record the book. Receive the credit. These simple statements extend freedom for our students to select independent reading, within the parameters of what our family considers acceptable, and earn credit. Keeping a cumulative reading list helps us integrate student-selected pleasure reads into high school courses.

A Reason to Celebrate

Colleges see, almost expect, a traditional approach to literature. I knew the traditional route would not work for my daughter's interest in Shakespeare. Literature could be more than a course to pass through. Instead we used an interest to drive learning.

Shakespeare wrote plays. Because plays are meant to be seen, not read, I took a unique approach to the study of this infamous author: watch, read, watch. After watching a performance at the professional Orlando Shakespeare Theater we would read the play. Once we read, we headed back to the theater to watch again. Having watched and read, then watching again, we comprehended the writing.

We followed this pattern over and over experiencing all of Shakespeare's major works and some of his minor lesser known, about twenty in total. Together we ushered for productions and my daughter earned community service hours while learning. At the end of the study, the student read The Complete Works of Shakespeare. *Shakespeare was no longer a foreign language; his works were understood, and enjoyed.*

Not only did we learn but this was not an expensive curriculum. We never paid to see a single production, and The Complete Works of Shakespeare *was purchased at a local bookstore for five dollars. Not a bad deal to experience one of history greatest playwrights.*

At one point in my daughter's high school career, she pondered taking a class on a high school campus. We met with the guidance counselor, transcript and paperwork in hand. Looking at the reading list, the guidance counselor questioned, "You read all these Shakespearean works? I never met a student who read more than two." The guidance counselor was immediately hooked to learn more about my daughter. When she decided not to attend, the counselor and English teacher were both disappointed. They knew my daughter would spur on the class.

Each high schooler in our family maintains a high school reading list of titles and authors on the computer. If the student reads excerpts from a book, he or she makes note in parenthesis. Once a book is recorded, it is easily copied from the list and pasted into an appropriate course description. The student's completed high school reading list is included in every college admission packet we submit. A sample reading list is included in this book on page 109.

Trying to interweave history and literature studies? We do, too! For example, we generally study American history simultaneously with American literature giving our students a deeper appreciation for the historic figures, notable events, or cultural influences of the times. Likewise, world history is studied alongside world literature. Our students are assigned or choose titles from the literature lists I compiled while researching recommended literature for college bound, high school students.

Teachers, textbook companies, and scholars often disagree as to which pieces of literature should be taught in which class. Ultimately, our students read a selection for its literary or historical value, not because it falls into a predetermined category. Intention is more important than category. My list, on page 102 is a springboard for the student's independent reading selections.

The reading list is long. Don't panic! No student will be able to read all the books. Families should choose the titles they feel are most appropriate, weighing concept to content and convictions. Note the list does not contain primary source documents or poetry, both important historical and literary genres which should be studied. Adding additional reading resources or a good anthology to include these genres is wise.

CAUTION: **Many of the literature pieces have adult themes or situations, please research the selection before assigning it to your student.**

The selections marked with an * are the titles most often recommended for advanced placement or college-bound students. Again, lists will vary. And, more wonderful books are published. When in doubt, check the College Board website or compare with other recommended reading lists.

American Literature

Alcott, Louisa May, *Little Men*

Alcott, Louisa May, *Little Women*

Barton, David, *Bulletproof George Washington*

Baum, L. Frank, *The Wizard of Oz*

Bierce, Ambrose, *Civil War Stories*

*Cather, Willa, *My Antonia*

*Cather, Willa, *O Pioneers!*

*Cooper, James Fenimore, *The Last of the Mohicans*

Crane, Stephen, *The Red Badge of Courage*

de Tocqueville, Alexis, *Democracy in America*

Dewey, John, *Democracy and Education*

*Douglass, Frederick, *Narrative of the Life of Frederick Douglass*

Edwards, Jonathan, *Sinners in the Hands of an Angry God*

*Faulkner, William, *The Sound and the Fury*

Fitzgerald, F. Scott, *The Great Gatsby*

Franklin, Benjamin, *The Autobiography of Benjamin Franklin*

Grafton, John, *The Declaration of Independence and Other Great Documents of American History*

Hawthorne, Nathaniel, *The Great Stone Face*

*Hawthorne, Nathaniel, *The Scarlet Letter*

*Hemingway, Earnest, *A Farewell to Arms*

*Hemingway, Earnest, *For Whom the Bell Tolls*

*Hemingway, Earnest, *The Old Man and the Sea*

*Hemingway, Earnest, *The Sun Also Rises*

*Hurston, Zora Neale, *Their Eyes Were Watching God*

Irving, Washington, *The Legend of Rip Van Winkle*

Irving, Washington, *The Legend of Sleepy Hollow*

Keller, Helen, *The Story of My Life*

*Lee, Harper, *To Kill a Mockingbird*

London, Jack, *The Sea-Wolf*

McCullough, David, *1776*

McCullough, David, *John Adams*

McCullough, David, *The Wright Brothers*

*Melville, Herman, *Moby Dick*

Miller, Arthur, *The Crucible*

Miller, Arthur, *The Death of a Salesman*

Rawlings, Marjorie Kinnan, *The Yearling*

O.Henry, short stories, *The Gift of the Magi*

Steinbeck, John, *Of Mice and Men*

*Steinbeck, John, *The Grapes of Wrath*

*Stowe, Harriet Beecher, *Uncle Tom's Cabin*

*Thoreau, Henry David, *Civil Disobedience*

*Thoreau, Henry David, *Walden*
Thurber, James, *The Secret Life of Walter Mitty*

Twain, Mark, *Life on the Mississippi*

Washington, Booker T., *Up From Slavery*

*Wilder, Thornton, *Our Town*

*Williams, Tennessee, *The Glass Menagerie*

Ancient World Literature

Aeschylus, *Prometheus Bound*

Aristotle, *Complete Works*

*Augustine, *Confessions*

*Augustine, *The City of God*

Baker, G. P., *Hannibal*

Bebe, The Venerable, *Ecclesiastical History of the English People*

Cicero, *Orations*

Epic of Gilgamesh

Euripides, *Medea*

Euripides, *Orestes*

Gibbon, Edward, *The Decline and Fall of the Roman Empire*

Graves, Robert, *Claudius, the God*

Graves, Robert, *I, Claudius: From the Autobiography of Tiberius Claudius*

Green, Roger Lancelyn, *Tales of Ancient Egypt*

Hamilton, Edith, *Mythology*

Hamilton, Edith, *The Greek Way*

Hamilton, Edith, *The Roman Way*

*Homer, *The Iliad*

*Homer, *The Odyssey*

Herodotus, *History of the Persian War*

Hippocrates, *Medical Writings*

Langford, Alan, *Tales of the Greek Heroes*

Ovid, *Metamorphoses*, translated by Rolfe Humphries

*Plato, *The Death of Socrates*

*Plato, *The Republic*

Plutarch, *Lives of Noble Grecians and Romans*

Seven Famous Greek Plays, edited by Whitney J. Oates and Eugene O'Neill, Jr.

*Shakespeare, William, *Antony and Cleopatra*

*Shakespeare, William, *Julius Caesar*

*Sophocles, *Antigone*

*Sophocles, *Oedipus Rex (Oedipus the King)*

*Sophocles, *Oedipus at Colonus*

Thucydides, *History of the Peloponnesian War*

Thucydides, *The Funeral Oration of Pericles*

Virgil, *The Aeneid*

Wallace, Lew, *Ben Hur*

British Literature

*Austen, Jane, *Pride and Prejudice*

Bacon, Francis, *Advancement of Learning*

Bacon, Francis, *Essays*

Blackstone, William, *Commentaries on the Laws of England*

Boswell, James, *The Life of Samuel Johnson*

*Bronte, Charlotte, *Jane Eyre*

*Bronte, Charlotte, *The Professor*

*Bronte, Emily, *Wuthering Heights*

*Bunyan, John, *The Pilgrim's Progress*

*Chaucer, Geoffrey, *The Canterbury Tales*

Chesterton, G.K., *Favorite Father Brown Stories*

Coleridge, Samuel Taylor, *Kubla Khan*

*Conrad, Joseph, *The Heart of Darkness*

Cranmer, Thomas, *The Book of Common Prayer*

Defoe, Daniel, *Robinson Crusoe*

*Dickens, Charles, *A Tale of Two Cities*

*Dickens, Charles, *Bleak House*

*Dickens, Charles, *David Copperfield*

*Dickens, Charles, *Great Expectations*

*Dickens, Charles, *Oliver Twist*

*Dickens, Charles, *Pickwick Papers*

Doyle, Sir Arthur Conan, *Sherlock Holmes*

Edwards, Jonathan, *Sinners in the Hands of an Angry God*

*Eliot, George, *Adam Bede*

*Eliot, George *Mill on the Floss*

*Eliot, George *Silas Marner*

Elizabeth I, Queen, *The Doubt of Future Foes*

Foxe, John, *The Book of Martyrs*

*Hardy, Thomas, *Far from the Maddening Crowd*

Huxley, Aldous, *Brave New World*

*Jonson, Ben, *Every Man in His Humor*

*Jonson, Ben, *The Alchemist*

*Jonson, Ben, *Volpone*

Kipling, Rudyard, *Captains Courageous*

Langland, William, *Piers Plowman*

Lewis, C. S., *Mere Christianity*

Lewis, C. S., *The Screwtape Letters*

Lewis, C.S., *Till We Have Faces*

*Locke, John, *An Essay Concerning Human Understanding*

Malory, Thomas, *Morte D'Arthur*

Marlowe, Christopher, *Tamburlaine*

Marlowe, Christopher, *The Jew of Malta*

Marlowe, Christopher, *The Tragical History of the Life and Death of Doctor Faustus*

Maugham, Somerset, *Of Human Bondage*

*Milton, John, *Paradise Lost*

*Milton, John, *Paradise Regained*

* Milton, John, *Samson Agonistes*

More, Sir Thomas, *Utopia*

Nordhoff, Charles, *Mutiny on the Bounty*

*Orwell, George, *Animal Farm*

Pyle, Howard, *Merry Adventures of Robin Hood*

Scott, Sir Walter, *Ivanhoe*

*Shakespeare, William, *A Midsummer Night's Dream*

*Shakespeare, William, *As You Like It*

*Shakespeare, William, *Hamlet*

*Shakespeare, William, *King Henry V*

*Shakespeare, William, *King Lear*

*Shakespeare, William, *King Richard the Second*

*Shakespeare, William, *King Richard the Third*

*Shakespeare, William, *Macbeth*

*Shakespeare, William, *Measure for Measure*

*Shakespeare, William, *Much Ado About Nothing*

*Shakespeare, William, *Othello*

*Shakespeare, William, *Romeo and Juliet*

*Shakespeare, William, *The Comedy of Errors*

*Shakespeare, William, *The First Part of King Henry IV*

*Shakespeare, William, *The Second Part of King Henry IV*

*Shakespeare, William, *The Taming of the Shrew*

*Shakespeare, William, *The Tempest*

*Shakespeare, William, *The Winter's Tale*

Shaw, George Bernard, *Pygmalion*

*Shelley, Wolstonecraft Mary, *Frankenstein*

Spenser, Edmund, *The Faire Queen*

Stevenson, Robert Louis, *Dr. Jekyll and Mr. Hyde*

Stevenson, Robert Louis, *Kidnapped*

Stevenson, Robert Louis, *Treasure Island*

*Swift, Jonathan, *Gulliver's Travels*

Wells, H. G., *Time Machine*

Wells, H.G., *War of the Worlds*

Wesley, John, *The Works of John Wesley*

Whitefield, George, *George Whitefield's Journals*

*Woolf, Virginia, *Jacob's Room*

*Woolf, Virginia, *Mrs. Dalloway*

*Woolf, Virginia, *The Waves*

*Woolf, Virginia, *To The Lighthouse*

World Literature

a Kempis, Thomas, *The Imitation of Christ*

Beowulf

Boome, Corrie Ten, *The Hiding Place*

*Dante, *Divine Comedy*

*Dante, *Inferno*

*de Cervantes, Miquel, *Don Quixote*

Celebrate High School: Finish with Excellence

Dostoevsky, Feodor, *Crime and Punishment*

*Machiavelli, Niccolo, *The Prince*

Marx, Karl, *The Communist Manifesto*

*Orczy, Baroness Emmuska, *The Scarlet Pimpernel*

Pasternak, Boris, *Doctor Zhivago*

*Poe, Edgar Allan, short stories

*Remarque, Erich Maria, *All Quiet on the Western Front*

*Rostand, Edmond, *Cyrano de Bergerac*

Sir Gawain and the Green Knight

*Solzhenitsyn, Alexander, *A Day in the Life of Ivan Denisovich*

*Thackeray, William, *Vanity Fair*

Tolstoy, Leo, *War and Peace*

*Vern, Jules, *Around the World in Eighty Days*

Vern, Jules, *Journey to the Center of the Earth*

*Vern, Jules, *Twenty Thousand Leagues Under the Sea*

*Voltaire, *Candide*

Wilde, Oscar, *The Picture of Dorian Gray*

Sites for Literary Travel

Do and remember. Learning literature is no different than taking a field trip to the fire station. Students who can experience will understand. While traveling through on your next vacation or visit, take a moment to stop and see. Add spark to literature studies by walking where the authors walked, sitting where the authors wrote. Your family will learn and remember together!

California
Jack London- Glen Ellen, California (home and ranch)

Connecticut
Harriet Beecher Stowe – Hartford, Connecticut (home)
Mark Twain – Hartford, Connecticut (home)

Florida
Ernest Hemingway- Key West, Florida (home)
Marjorie Kinnan Rawlings- Cross Creek, Florida (home)

Illinois
Ernest Hemmingway – Oak Park, Illinois (birthplace)

Massachusetts
Louisa May Alcott- Concord, Massachusetts (Orchard House)
Thornton W. Burgess- Sandwich, Massachusetts (birthplace and home)
Emily Dickinson- Amherst, Massachusetts (home)
Ralph Waldo Emerson- Concord, Massachusetts (home)
Nathaniel Hawthorne – Salem, Massachusetts (birthplace), Concord, Massachusetts (home)
Henry Wadsworth Longfellow- Cambridge, Massachusetts (home)
Herman Melville- Pitsfield, Massachusetts (home)
Edgar Allen Poe – Boston, Massachusetts (birthplace)
Henry David Thoreau- Concord, Massachusetts (Walden Pond)

Minnesota
F. Scott Fitzgerald – St. Paul, Minnesota (birthplace)

Mississippi
William Faulkner- New Albany, Mississippi (birthplace), Oxford, Mississippi (home)

Missouri
Laura Ingalls Wilder- Mansfield, Missouri (home)
Mark Twain- Florida, Missouri (birthplace), Hannibal, Missouri (home)

New Hampshire
Robert Frost – Franconia, New Hampshire (home)

New York
Washington Irving- New York, New York (birthplace)
Edgar Allen Poe- The Bronx, New York (home)

High School Reading List for (Student Name)

2004-2005

Questions of the French Revolution, Jacques Sole
The Lost King of France, Deborah Cadbury
Paris in the Terror, Stanley Loomis
Last Citadel, David L. Robbins
The Scarlet Letter, Nathaniel Hawthorne
Silas Marner, George Eliot
The Jungle, Upton Sinclair
Cyrano de Bergerac, Edmond Rostand
To Kill a Mockingbird, Harper Lee
The Red Badge of Courage, Stephen Crane
The Hiding Place, Corrie ten Boom
Lord of the Flies, William Golding
The Adventures of Huckleberry Finn, Mark Twain
The Old Man and the Sea, Ernest Hemmingway
The Sun Also Rises, Ernest Hemmingway
Treasure Island, Robert Louis Stevenson
A Christmas Carol, Charles Dickens
The Giver, Lois Lowry
God Smuggler, Brother Andrew
The Cost of Discipleship, Dietrich Bonhoeffer
All Quiet on the Western Front, Erich Maria Rmarque

Record Keeping Tip

Why is a cumulative reading list important?

Maintaining a chronological reading is beneficial for many reasons:

- The reading list may be requested by some colleges for homeschooled applicants.
- The reading list helps to write course descriptions.
- The reading list adds depth to the student's education.
- The reading list reflects the student's interests.
- The reading list validates course content.
- A comprehensive reading list can make an impression. I know students who were accepted into colleges because of their reading list.
- The reading list can be used as a reference for younger siblings.

2005-2006

Babylon, Joan Oates (excerpts)
The Epic of Gilgamesh
Noah's Flood: New Scientific Discoveries about the Event that Changed History, William Ryan and Walter Pitman
The Quest for Sumer, Leonard Cottrell
Oedipus Rex, Sophocles
Oedipus at Colonus, Sophocles
Antigone, Sophocles
Mysteries of Ancient China, Jessica Rawson (excerpts)
Daily Life in Ancient Egypt, Waley-el-dine Sameh (excerpts)
People of the Sea: The Search for the Philistines, Trude and Moshe Dothan (excerpts)
Mythology, Edith Hamilton
The Death of Socrates, Plato
The Greek Way, Edith Hamilton
For the Temple, G.A. Henty
The Riddle of the Rosetta Stone: Keys to Ancient Egypt, Giblin
The Great Wall, Leonard Fisher
In the Footsteps of Alexander the Great, Michael Wood (excerpts)
The Republic, Plato, translated by G. M. A.Grube (excerpts)
The Young Carthaginian, G. A. Henty
The Roman Way, Edith Hamilton (excerpts)
Eagle of the Ninth, Rosemary Sutcliff
I, Claudius: From the Autobiography of Tiberius Claudius, Robert Graves
Claudius the God, Robert Graves
Hannibal, G. P. Baker

(Student Name) High School Reading List- page 1

Pitiless Parodies and Other Outrageous Verse, Frank Jacobs
Don Quixote, Cervantes

2006-2007

Macbeth, William Shakespeare
Julius Caesar, William Shakespeare
Romeo and Juliet, William Shakespeare
Canterbury Tales, Geoffrey Chaucer
Dr. Faustus, Christopher Marlowe
Paradise Lost, John Milton
Robinson Crusoe, Daniel DeFoe
Lord of the Rings, J. R. R. Tolkien
Sir Gawain and the Green Knight
The Faerie Queen, Edmund Spenser
Kidnapped, Robert Louis Stevenson
The Prince and the Pauper, Mark Twain
Great Expectations, Charles Dickens (excerpts)
Tale of Two Cities, Charles Dickens (excerpts)
Gift of the Magi, O. Henry
Gulliver's Travels, Jonathan Swift
Frankenstein, Mary Shelley
The Picture of Dorian Gray, Oscar Wilde
A Year with C.S. Lewis: Daily Readings from His Classic Works, C. S. Lewis
The Invisible Man, H.G. Wells
Till We Have Faces, C.S. Lewis
The Innocence of Father Brown, G.K. Chesterton
The Screwtape Letters, C.S. Lewis
1984, George Orwell

2007-2008

How to Win Friends and Influence People, Dale Carnegie
Seven Men Who Rule the World From the Grave, Dave Breese
Parenting From the Heart, Marilyn Boyer
World Religions, Susan Meredith
Good to Great, Jim Collins
John Adams, David McCullough
Tuesdays With Morrie, Mitch Albom
East of Eden, John Steinbeck
Lessons from the Top: The Search for America's Best Business Leaders, Thomas J. Neff and James M. Citrin
What's So Amazing About Grace? Philip Yancy
Blue Like Jazz, Donald Miller
The Hungering Dark, Frederick Buechner
A Day in the Life of Ivan Denisovich, Alexander Solzhenitsyn
The Pearl, John Steinbeck
The Saving Life of Christ, Major Ian Thomas
The Green Letters: Principles of Spiritual Growth, Miles J. Stanford
Do Hard Things, Alex and Brett Harris
Proving the Unseen, George MacDonald
Simply Christian, N. T. Wright
Why We Aren't Emergent by Two Guys Who Should Be, Kevin DeYoung and Ted Kluck

Whether writing a resume or completing a college application, your student will be asked to detail time allotted to activities outside scholastic studies. We created a spreadsheet file to document how our students spend their time. Each student can record the required information as activities are completed. On our spreadsheet we record the name of the organization and supervisor's name, contact phone number, activity dates, hours spent on the activity, and a short description of what the activity entailed. This information helped to write essays for college admission as well as resumes for potential employers. This is the document my oldest son kept of his activities.

Co-curricular Involvement- (Student Name)

Varsity Baseball   **80 hours per month**   **1 year to present**
Played year-round baseball with additional conditioning, weight and speed training, lettering Spring 2007, and anticipating playing and lettering Spring 2008.

JV Baseball   **72 hours per month**   **2 years**
Played year-round baseball with additional conditioning, weight and speed training during the freshman and sophomore years.

Youth Group   **12 hours per month**   **2 years**
Participated in church youth group, with one year of student leadership.

OCC   **12 hours per month**   **4 months**
Volunteered as a community partner and mentor for at-risk children in the Orlando area.

Assistant Instructor-Baseball **20 hours for one week**   **2 seasons**
Volunteered as a coach's assistant, instructor, and mentor for younger ball players.

Competitive Gaming   **35 hours per month**   **1 year**
Elected team leader of 36 players for *Command and Conquer III*; ranked 32 internationally for *Star Wars Empire at War*.

Stock Market Game   **4 hours per month**   **1 year**
Won the Stock Market Game as part of the economics class, doubling the initial investment in one year.

Concession Stand Volunteer **20 hours per month**   **3 months**
Supervised concession stand operations and volunteers.

Community service has multi-faceted value: potential growth of the student's character, enhancement of academic subject matter, knowledge of life skills, and possibilities for scholarship eligibility. We found community service to be life-impacting for our students. One student developed a passion to help families living in poverty. Today he is the CFO of an organization which works to create sustainability in the education and business structure of Haiti.

Many states require community service hours for state merit scholarships. Research requirements for your state when your student enters eighth grade with the intention of encouraging him or her to start service in ninth grade. If service is not required for state merit scholarships, consider setting time aside for these experiences as colleges consider ways the student impacted their communities of influence when her or she applies for **FL** admission.

Florida requires specified hours of community service for Bright Futures scholarship. The particulars of how and where the student may serve will depend on where the student is registered for high school. If the student is registered with a nontraditional private school, the student should contact the guidance counselor inquiring where the service can be completed and how the hours must be recorded. If the student is registered with the county home education program, the student must have hours verified on letterhead from the agency at which the hours were served. If you live outside of Florida, research the specifics for your state.

I have found the easiest way to have hours documented is to request a letter from the student's supervisor as soon as possible after the service is completed. When collecting verification of my student's hours, I draft a letter containing all the details needed and the email the pre-written document to the supervisor requesting the letter be printed on letterhead and signed. Doing the "legwork" for the company ensured I would get the information I needed and that it would be returned in a timely manner. Once the letter was received, I placed it in a plastic protective sleeve and added it to the cumulative high school folder.

NOTE: State merit scholarship requirements change. Stay informed and stay current.

We use the template below making sure to include the body of the letter or letterhead includes the name, address, and phone number of the venue, the supervisor's name and contact information, the dates and hours the student served, and the work the student performed. I use the same template for every high school student, editing as necessary.

July 1, 2014
To Whom It May Concern:

This letter verifies that (student name) worked (the number of total hours) hours of community service for (name of organization) from (dates). (Student name) served as a (description of the activity) and received no monetary compensation for the work completed.

Sincerely,
(Supervisor's name)

Once the needed information is inserted into the letter, it is emailed to the supervisor with a warm thank you for giving our student the opportunity to serve at the organization.

Thank you for allowing our daughter, Sally Smith, volunteer at the East Summerfield Preschool Art Camp. She thoroughly enjoyed using her creativity while working with your talented teachers.

The hours Sally served must be documented for scholarship purposes. I have drafted a verification letter with the required information in an effort to respect your time. Please print the attached letter on the official letterhead of your school. I will come by the school and pick up the hard copy at your convenience. My contact number is 000-000-0000.

The final letter, printed on letterhead, with all the pertinent information is concise and informative.

July 1, 2014

To Whom It May Concern:

This letter verifies Sally Smith volunteered 24 total hours of community service for East Summerfield Preschool from June 5, 2014 through June 20, 2014. Sally served as a teen helper, assisting the teacher and helping three- and five-year-old children complete art projects. Sally received no monetary compensation for her service with us.

Sincerely,

Jane R. Jones
Director, East Summerfield Preschool

Letters of recommendation are written and submitted by a third party who can attest to the academic accomplishments, work ethic, and personal character of a student. Every college will require letters of recommendation for admission, however each will request the letters from different sources. Sources most often required by colleges are teachers (online, co-op, professors), band directors, art instructors, employers, supervisors, youth pastors, senior pastors, and coaches.

As your student enters ninth grade, be mindful of the people from which you may want to request letters. Do the same for tenth, eleventh, and twelfth grades. As opportunities become evident, request a letter. Letters written when the information is fresh will be more accurate and therefore, more effective. Once the letters are received, place them in protective sleeves and file chronologically in the student's cumulative high school notebook.

We have had several occasions to need a recommendation prior to applying to college. Thankfully we had a letter on hand. For our circumstances we did not need any of the details of the letter changed. However, some letters need to be specific for a purpose. If details do need to be changed to meet the needs of a request or job position, contact the person who wrote the recommendation, scan a copy of the original, and ask them graciously to adjust the letter. I have been asked to do this several times for letters I have written and was thrilled to oblige. Often the person writing the letter has such respect and admiration for the young adult that he or she is honored to make the adjustment.

When contemplating who may be able to write a letter for your student, consider the examples below:

- Your ninth grade daughter, Emily, earns first chair in the youth symphony. The director congratulates Emily and comments on her musical talent and her work ethic. Two weeks later, the director invites Emily to compete at federation. She prepares, competes, and receives a superior rating. The director continues to speak highly of Emily's work ethic and musical talent. You decide to ask the band director to write a letter of recommendation for Emily which addresses her work ethic and musical abilities.

- Tyson, your eleventh grade son, is a student leader for his youth group, responsible for facilitating a middle school Bible study, coordinating service projects, and promoting weekly activities. He accompanied the middle school youth on a summer mission trip. The university to which Tyson is applying has asked for a recommendation from a guidance counselor, which does not apply to Tyson's high school experience. You call the college admissions department inquiring how to comply with their request. Admissions asks if Tyson is involved in church activities and agrees to allow a pastor to write a recommendation which speaks for Tyson's maturity, leadership, integrity, and motivation.

- Your twelfth grade daughter is applying to a highly selective college which is requesting a letter of recommendation written by a teacher from a currently enrolled class. The student is completing independent studies at home but is enrolled in an online Spanish course from an accredited school. You call the college admissions office and explain the scenario. They request the online instructor complete the recommendation portion of the application.

When asking someone to write a letter of recommendation, be specific as to which character or academic qualities you would like addressed. Be sure the person writing the letter can evaluate those traits. Traits to consider may include initiative, motivation, work habits, punctuality, self-confidence, concern for others, integrity, maturity, discipline, and leadership.

My students or I request letters of recommendation in person, face to face, whenever possible. There have been several occasions when this was not feasible. In those situations we either email a request or make a phone call. A copy of the letter may be similar to the one below:

Dear Mrs. Evans,

I am applying to State University this fall. The admissions office is requiring that I submit a letter of recommendation from someone who can verify my academic abilities and achievements. Specifically they are looking for information regarding my ability to express my thoughts in writing, to contribute to class discussion, to be disciplined in study habits, to respect faculty, and to exhibit academic integrity. As my English instructor for the past two years, I knew you would be able to most accurately represent my abilities. I would be honored if you would write a letter on my behalf, addressed to Dr. Stanley Straight, Dean of Admissions, State University, 123 First Avenue, City, State, 12345. Thank you in advance your time.

Sincerely,
Natalie Short

Colleges may have special instructions regarding who should write the letters, when the letters can be written, and how the letters should be submitted. Pay close attention to these instructions. Admissions personnel are not impressed when directions are not followed as they request. If you have questions, make a phone call or send an email.

Our son applied to a college which required one letter of recommendation to be submitted by a teacher from the senior year. Another college asked for a form to be submitted by a guidance counselor. Each of these scenarios posed dilemmas for our home educated student. We called the admissions offices to inquire about how we could meet their requirements. Both offices were understanding and warmly offered alternatives. The first college allowed an online instructor to write a letter and the second college suggested our youth pastor complete the form and submit it via sealed envelope.

As with any high school records, make copies of the originals. When an important paper entered our home, I immediately made several copies and placed them in a protective sleeve with the original. Originals were reserved for college admission or employment. When we needed a form I pulled out the cumulative folder and selected what we needed. This discipline saved us time and energy.

Sample Letter of Recommendation
(This is an actual letter written to recommend a student for admission. The names have been changed.)

Beth Recommender
123 School Street
Anywhere, ME 00000
(000)000-0000

To Whom It May Concern:

Dedicated, motivated, goal-oriented, determined, and driven are all words that describe Sarah Student. Sarah is a strong student with a drive and determination that often astounds most who have the privilege to teach, coach, and mentor her. Every project, every paper, and assignment was done with enthusiasm and integrity. Sarah puts her best into all that life sets before her. She sets goals and moves toward them. When she was a freshmen, he began her first novel, a historical fiction piece about the Revolutionary War. The quality of her work was outstanding. Her ability to retain knowledge, to write with skill, and her ability to communicate ideas have been strong suits for her.

Sarah is a self-motivated, self-disciplined young lady. She is an independent thinker, but also knows how to apply learned theories and ideas. She is strong-willed and knows when and how to take initiative. This young lady will attack her college and professional career just as she has her high school education, with vigor and fortitude. If she uses half of what I have had the privilege of seeing she will be a great success in anything she chooses to attack.

The best part about Sarah is not what she knows or what skills she has, but what she does with it. She is determined to be a woman of integrity. She is honest, hard-working, and compassionate. She cares for people, her family, her team, her friends, and her community. Whatever path this young lady takes, it will not only be done well, but with impeccable character.

With great pleasure I whole-heartedly recommend Miss Sarah Student for your school.

Sincerely yours,

Beth Recommender
Teacher

Sample Letter of Recommendation
(This is an actual letter written to recommend a student for admission. The names have been changed.)

(Name of college) Office of Admission
1000 University Avenue
Collegeville, FL 00000

December 2, 2014

To Whom It May Concern:

I am writing this letter of recommendation for Samuel Student, currently enrolled in my Spanish II course with the (name of school). Our student-teacher relationship is not in the traditional sense because of the online learning venue. Hence, our interactions are frequent and include email correspondence as well as phone assessments.

During the time I have worked with Samuel, he has demonstrated responsibility by submitting all assignments either on time or ahead of schedule. He has always performed above average academically and my conversations with him lead me to believe he does this with all his courses. Samuel further distinguishes himself as a dedicated individual because he takes the imitative to do his work. Because my class is an online course there is no face-to-face contact and no overt pressure for him to do the work on time. In this environment, the teacher is only there when the student enters the online course. Students must have self discipline to succeed in this environment. Samuel consistently contacts me to do oral components of the course or to complete the parent phone calls. He takes full responsibility for his learning.

Because we talk frequently there has been the opportunity to know Samuel on a personal level and he is actively involved in sports. I have learned that he takes an interest in the stock market and wishes to pursue a career in international business. His knowledge of Spanish will certainly assist him in that endeavor. In the past few months, I have come to understand that Samuel is motivated to achieve above average goals and shows great intellectual promise. I have no doubt that he will succeed at a high level and am confident that he will be a great asset to the (name) College student body.

Please do not hesitate to contact me if you need more information regarding this exceptional student.

Sincerely,

Vivianne Spanish Instructor
Instructor, Spanish II
(name of school)
000-000-0000

Sample Letter of Recommendation
(This is an actual letter written to recommend a student for admission for an honors college. The names have been changed.)

March 4, 2014

(Name), Director, The Honors Institute
(Name) College
1000 University Avenue
Collegeville, FL 00000

Ms. Director,

Ambitious, motivated, and driven describe Samuel Student. Having been introduced to Samuel as an inquisitive kindergarten child and meeting yearly thereafter to evaluate his academic progress as a home educated student, my husband, a Florida certified teacher, and I have had the privilege of watching Samuel mature academically and personally, growing through challenges to become the confident, resolute, articulate young adult he is today. Samuel is a well-rounded young man of excellent character.

As a home educated student, Samuel was afforded and seized every opportunity to learn new concepts and skills. Every summer Samuel enthusiastically shared what he had learned as well as what he envisioned for his coming school year. One year he was determined to learn how to play the drums. Nine months later he gave a solo concert in our living room as part of his yearly evaluation. Samuel eagerly shared summaries of books he read, largely self-initiated. His knowledge of many subjects, as well as his character, was evident in his writing samples. From kindergarten through high school, Samuel was fortunate to experience a variety of learning environments, from independent study to interactive cooperatives. Academically, Samuel surpasses his peers.

Samuel never lacks motivation; learning for him is intrinsic and he consistently feeds his inquiring, curious mind. He reads engaging literature, interacts with people of all ages and cultures, and volunteers in his community and church; hence Samuel is a proficient communicator with adept interpersonal skills. Samuel is also an athlete competing in baseball and weightlifting, receiving the Sportsmanship Award in 2011. As a musician, Samuel has played in the marching, concert, and jazz bands while also serving as a mentor to beginner percussionists in his church. These skills, coupled with his work ethic and determination, will be of great advantage as he furthers his education, first through dual enrollment and later as he pursues his goal of attending The United States Military Academy, West Point.

Samuel is an exceptional young man who will succeed in any endeavor he pursues. Currently, Samuel is a full-time home education student who actively serves as First Lieutenant and Flight Commander in the JROTC at his districted high school. He was recently accepted into the Kitty Hawk Air Honors Society.

Based on my knowledge of the person Samuel Student is, which includes his outstanding academic record, it is without reservation I recommend him be admitted to (Name) Honors Institute at (Name) College. He will be an asset to the campus and represent the college well.

Sincerely Yours,

Beth Recommender

Colleges require applicants to submit essays, writing samples, or personal statements with their admission packet. Essay topics can often be found on the college website or on the college application. Researching and practicing essay writing before actually submitting an actual application is helpful and recommended.

Some colleges have a word count requirement for their essays. Therefore, students may benefit from writing practice with a specific word count. For example, a parent may ask the student to write a 500 word essay about what he or she will contribute to the first choice college campus.

Our first son practiced his essay writing during the first nine weeks. He would write the essay, we would edit together, and he would rewrite. Once he was satisfied with the essay, he printed two copies, filing one in his yearly portfolio of work samples and the other in the cumulative notebook. Writing essays was a rewarding exercise, as our student had a vested interest in the final product.

Parents, get ready to write. You, too, may be required to submit addendums to college applications. When our son applied to a highly selective college, I was required to write several essays detailing our educational philosophy and evaluation methods. Frustrated at first, I soon realized the personal value of the requirement. I had to think, really ponder, why we did what we did. It was helpful to remind myself of the value of our years of hard work. In the end, as we graduated our son, I found writing those essays one of the most introspective experiences of my homeschooling journey. I was able to embrace our son's milestone in a tangible manner.

Sports Videos

Our home educated sons played high school baseball on the local public school team. Though both had aspired to play ball at the college level, neither decided not to pursue their dream. However, we know several players who did go on to play college or professional sports. Many of those athletes needed video clips of their play, in a variety of situations and positions on the field, to submit to colleges and scouts. If your student wants to play collegiate or professional sports, inquire whether this documentation is something you will need.

Florida home educated students registered with their county superintendent are eligible to play high school sports with the public high school for which their residence is zoned. Home educated athletes must meet the immunization and GPA requirements required of public school athletes. Grade verification forms are required by the Florida High School Athletic Association. For more information, refer to Florida Statute Section 1006.15(5), named "The Craig Dickinson Act".

FL

Our boys played Little League baseball, competitive travel ball, and had a desire to play at the college level. When each student entered the eighth grade, I bookmarked the NCAA website and visited the site two times a year to stay current on requirements and deadlines. I also read any articles—from HSLDA, my state publication, and home education magazines—I could get my hands on. Talking with parents who had been through the collegiate sports experience was also helpful. Having heard the NCAA requirements for home educated students were arduous I wanted to "stay on top of my game".

The NCAA website contains a wealth of information for students who want to pursue sports in college.

• Students educated at home for any part of high school (grades nine through twelve) intending to play collegiate sports, must register with the NCAA Eligibility Center **during the junior year**.

> Register with the Eligibility Center
>
> 🖥 http://web1.ncaa.org/ECWR2/NCAA_EMS/NCAA_EMS.html?test=1#
>
> The NCAA provides a very helpful home school check list. This resource help parents stay organized.
>
> 🖥http://fs.ncaa.org/Docs/eligibility_center/Student_Resources
> Home_School_Checklist.pdf
>
> The Initial Eligibility standards will be changing for the Class of 2016 and beyond. Be sure to keep up with the changes taking place.
>
> 🖥 http://fs.ncaa.org/Docs/eligibility_center/Quick_Reference_Sheet.pdf

• The NCAA prepared a helpful Home School Information guide.

> 🖥 http://fs.ncaa.org/Docs/eligibility_center/Student_Resources/
> Home_School_Information.pdf

• Verifying which core courses are required by the NCAA is essential. As stated on the website "for Division I, generally only courses completed in grades nine through twelve may be considered core courses. One core-course unit taken in summer school after the eighth semester may not be used to meet the core-course requirements. In Division II, a student may use all core courses taken prior to initial, full-time collegiate enrollment to meet the core-curriculum requirement, including a core course taken in summer school after grade twelve."

- College courses taken during high school can be used to meet the core-course requirements **if** the course is included on the home school transcript and would meet the requirements for a core course. Sixteen core courses are required for Division I and fourteen core courses for Division II. **Note: These requirements change. Please research current requirements.**

  Acceptable core titles

  💻 https://web1.ncaa.org/eligibilitycenter/student/index_student.html

- **College courses taken in the eighth grade** or by credit-by-exam will not be accepted as a core course.

- Contact

  NCAA Eligibility Center (Atten: Home School Evaluation)
  1802 Alonzo Watford Sr. Drive
  Indianapolis, IN 46202-6222
  Telephone: 1-877-262-1492

A Reason to Celebrate

The NCAA course description sheets asked for very specific information in addition to what was covered in the course. It required that I list how grades were calculated and who taught the student the information and administered the grade. They only required specific courses (core courses) to be submitted. Although it was detailed and rigorous, the website was very clear in exactly how to present the information. They were a homeschool parent's dream in that respect.

Be familiar with admission requirements for colleges of interest and work to meet those requirements. Recheck test score requirements each school year to be sure the requirements have not changed. Waiting until the senior year is too late.

Students who plan to attend a four-year college after high school graduation may be required to take the SAT and/or the ACT. Colleges generally have a minimum test score required for admission, though a growing number of colleges are test optional. In addition to SAT and ACT, some colleges require students to take the SAT Subject Tests (formerly SAT II Subject Tests). When registering for the PSAT, SAT or the ACT, a six-digit school code will be required. Homeschool codes are in the call-out blasts. If the student is registered with a non-traditional private school, contact the school for their code.

- **PSAT (Preliminary SAT, National Merit Scholarship Qualifying Test)**

The new PSAT (as of October 2015) is a three-part test preparing students for the SAT and determining qualification for National Merit Scholarship. It is not a college entrance exam. Students can sit for the PSAT in their **sophomore** and **junior** year, however, the score earned on the PSAT during the **junior** year determines qualification for National Merit Scholarship. The score may also be used to determine eligibility for other scholarships as well. The PSAT is administered once a year, in October. The test takes two hours and forty-five minutes to complete. Registration is through the local high school or private school offering the test. The homeschool school code is 991099.

- **SAT**

Currently (May 2015), the SAT is a three-part reasoning test measuring critical reading, mathematics and timed essay writing. The test is offered seven times a year. Students register through the College Board website and take the SAT at a designated testing center, generally a local public high school. It is wise to plan ahead as registration fees increase closer to testing. Scores on each test range from 200-800. All three parts are taken in the same sitting, however, scores from different sittings can be "mixed and matched" when determining the total score. For example, at his first sitting, Stan scored a 620 on critical reading, a 550 on mathematics, and a 500 on writing. At his second sitting, Stan scored a 610 in critical reading, a 590 on mathematics, and a 475 on writing. The highest scores from each sub-section would be totaled to determine admission eligibility. Though some colleges use only the critical reading and mathematics scores for admission, others add the writing score. Be familiar with the testing requirements for colleges of interest. The homeschool school code is 970000.

The SAT is being redesigned and will be the only SAT format offered after March 2016. On the new SAT students can expect to find a reading test, a writing and language test, a math test, and an essay. **The scoring will be different than the former SAT.**

- https://collegereadiness.collegeboard.org/sat (information on the new SAT)
- https://collegereadiness.collegeboard.org/sat/scores

• SAT Subject Tests

The SAT Subject Tests are content-based tests offered numerous times during the year, but not every test is offered at every sitting. Check the College Board website testing schedule for details. Colleges, especially highly selective universities, may require three to five subject tests in addition to the SAT and ACT. In fact, some colleges require more SAT II tests from homeschooled students than public school students. Currently there are 20 tests available in five subject areas: literature, mathematics, history, sciences, and world languages. Plan ahead, checking with college admissions to verify which tests they require. Students should take subject tests as they complete study in the content area as the test is very detailed and subject-specific. The administration time for each subject-specific test is one hour. SAT Subject Tests are usually taken in eleventh or twelfth grade.

Tests available

Literature	U.S. History	World History	Math Level I
Math Level II	Biology	Chemistry	Physic
French	French with Listening	German with Listening	German
Spanish	Spanish with Listening	Modern Hebrew	Italian
Korean with Listening	Chinese with Listening	Japanese with Listening	Latin

🖥 https://sat.collegeboard.org/about-tests/sat-subject-tests

• ACT

The ACT, offered six times a year, is a four-part achievement test measuring knowledge in math, English, reading and science with an optional timed writing component. Not all colleges require the writing component. Each of the four parts are scored from 1 to 36 and the scores are then averaged to obtain a composite score. The composite score is the score most colleges require. Home educated students should use 969-999 for the school code.

🖥 http://www.actstudent.org/testprep/descriptions/
🖥 https://apstudent.collegeboard.org/apcourse

• The PERT

The PERT—Postsecondary Education Readiness Test—measures how prepared a student is for postsecondary education. The three-part assessment is computer-adaptive—questions are computer-generated based on the previous question—with the results intended to help place students in classes where they will be most successful. Each section of the test is thirty questions. The test is not timed.

🖥 http://www.fldoe.org/schools/higher-ed/fl-college-system/common-
        placement-testing.stml
🖥 http://www.fldoe.org/core/fileparse.php/5592/urlt/0078248-pert-
        studentstudyguide.pdf (study guide)
🖥 http://wchs.pasco.k12.fl.us/wp-content/uploads/wchs/2012/01/pert-math-
        study-guide-1.pdf (study guide)

- **CLEP**

Often referred to as "testing-out", the College-Level Placement Examination Program (CLEP) developed by the College Board enables high school students to complete college-level independent study and earn college credit while in high school. Currently, there are thirty-three exams available, each test lasting from 90-120 minutes. Earning CLEP credit can also be a beneficial method of validating the student's ability to complete college-level course work. Students should inquire with colleges of choice to be sure the credit will be honored.

🖥 https://clep.collegeboard.org/started

CLEP Exams (available May 2015)

Business
Financial Accounting
Information Systems and Computer
      Applications
Introductory Business Law
Principles of Management
Principles of Marketing

History & Social Science
Principles of Macroeconomics
Principles of Microeconomics
American Government
History of the United States I
History of the United States II
Western Civilization I
Western Civilization II
Social Sciences and History
Human Growth and Development
Introduction to Educational Psychology
Introductory Psychology
Introductory Sociology

English
American Literature
English Literature
Analyzing and Interpreting Literature
College Composition
College Composition Modular
Humanities

World Languages & Cultures
French Language — Levels 1 and 2
German Language — Levels 1 and 2
Spanish Language — Levels 1 and 2

Mathematics & Science
Precalculus
Calculus
College Algebra
College Mathematics
Biology
Chemistry
Natural Sciences

- **AP Exams**

Advanced Placement gives high school students opportunities to excel in college-level classes, earning college credit with thirty-six courses and exams. In an effort to make the exams available to all students, homeschooled high schoolers who do not have access to AP courses may take AP exams without taking the class. The subject-specific exams are two to three hours in length and are scored on a scale from one to five. Colleges award credit for scores of three and above depending on the course. Check with the AP policy of colleges of interest before taking AP courses. Not all colleges treat the credit in the same manner.

🖥 https://professionals.collegeboard.com/testing/ap/about
🖥 http://apcentral.collegeboard.com/apc/public/courses/index.html

Advance Placement (AP) Exams (available May 2015)

Math & Computer Science
AP Calculus AB (due to change 2016-2017)
AP Calculus BC (due to change 2016-2017)
AP Computer Science A
AP Statistics

History & Social Science
AP Comparative Government and Politics
AP European History (due to change 2015-2016)
AP Human Geography
AP Macroeconomics
AP Microeconomics
AP Psychology
AP United States Government and Politics
AP United States History
AP World History (due to change 2016-2017)

Sciences
AP Biology
AP Chemistry
AP Environmental Science
AP Physics C: Electricity and Magnetism
AP Physics C: Mechanics
AP Physics 1: Algebra-Based
AP Physics 2: Algebra-Based

English
AP English Language and Composition
AP English Literature and Composition

World Languages & Cultures
AP Chinese Language and Culture
AP French Language and Culture
AP German Language and Culture
AP Italian Language and Culture
AP Japanese Language and Culture
AP Latin
AP Spanish Language and Culture
AP Spanish Literature and Culture

Arts
AP Art History (due to change 2015-2016)*
AP Music Theory
AP Studio Art 2-D Design
AP Studio Art 3-D Design
AP Studio Art: Drawing

AP Capstone
AP Research (due to change 2015-2016)*
AP Seminar

Test Preparation

Students wanting to improve test scores must get to know the test. Students who prepare score higher. For test preparation, search the test name followed by "prep" for online resources including question-of-the-day emails and video tutorials. Printed materials are available in local libraries. Online classes are also available, but never underestimate the power and benefits of independent study. In some cases independent study proves more advantageous than expensive courses and tutoring.

Test preparation is as unique as a student's four-year plan. What works for one student may not work for another.

Notes

Chapter 8

Finishing Well

Rounding the bend, in the final stretch, the end is in sight. It will not be long and the tassel will be turned, the cap thrown in celebration of a journey finished well. These final moments can be bittersweet: thankful to be finished, saddened the journey is complete, joy-filled as the young adult spreads wings to fly.

Before we throw that final celebration, there are a few loose ends to tie: dual enrollment, affidavits, and diplomas.

Dual Enrollment

Dual enrollment courses—classes taken by high school students at a local college or university—give a student the ability to earn both high school and college credit, simultaneously. Juniors and seniors, and sometimes younger students, commonly take advantage of this option as a productive way to complete general education requirements in a small class setting with individualized instruction. However, parents and students may want to research professors and course content before enrolling.

Dual enrollment can validate a student's transcript, "proving" the student can complete college-level work. Tuition is generally free or greatly reduced, however the student may be required to purchase books. These stipulations vary from state to state.

⌨ www.fldoe.org/core/fileparse.php/5423/urlt/DualEnrollmentFAQ.pdf FL

Research professors and course content before enrolling. When the student completes a dual enrollment course, write a course description to be included with the student's high school course description paperwork. One parent submitted this course description:

Survey of English Literature	1.0 high school credit

The student completed all course requirements for this course while dual enrolled at Red Ridge State College. The completed course earned the student 1 high school credit and 3 college credits.

One of the most frequently asked questions regarding dual enrollment is how to determine what credits should be awarded to a high school student. The state of Florida has published a high school equivalency list. This list is an easy reference tool for parents.

🖥 http://www.fldoe.org/core/fileparse.php/7480/urlt/0082780-delist.pdf
(high school subject area equivalency list)

Parents and students must also consider the "Excess Credit Hour Surcharge". In 2012 the Legislature modified Section 1009.286 of the Florida Statute for students entering college Fall 2012 and later. The threshold percentage is now 110%. In other words, if the student is seeking a degree requiring 120 credits the student will be subject to an excess credit surcharge for any credit taken after 132 hours. All credit hours taken by the student in college apply toward the threshold, even courses which the student failed, withdrew, repeated, transferred, or dropped after add/drop. Credits earned by means of AP, IB or dual enrollment do not count toward the "Excess Credit Hour Surcharge". There are a few other credit circumstances which are exempt. Further research is needed by parents and students considering this option.

Students registered with a nontraditional private school should discuss their questions regarding dual enrollment with a guidance counselor as an articulation agreement may be required. Students registered with their county home education program should contact the dual enrollment counselor at the college. Enrollment requirements, including minimum age, grade point averages, transcripts, college-entrance exams, and placement scores, vary from college to college, as well as by legislative session. Another area to stay up-to-date, but the effort may save the student money.

What If High School Does Not Go As Planned?

Not accepted at the college of choice.
Employer hired someone else.
A test score lower than hoped.

There are no guarantees.

Circumstances do not always turn out as we had hoped or planned. Doubts flood our minds. Maybe we should not have home schooled? If we had sent her to public school for her foreign language, it would have been accepted. Should we have taken more practice tests? We second guess our decisions and head into a downward spiral with no way out. The truth is, even if we had done things differently, had made other choices, there would have been no guarantees.

Homeschooling families are not the only ones facing disappointment. I have known International Baccalaureate students in public schools who stayed up the majority of the night studying week after week and still did not get into their first choice colleges. Should they have been in another school? Should have they have been home educated? Even public school parents second guess their choices.

When our oldest son was applying to colleges, he decided last minute he wanted to submit application to a college with excessive admission requirements for home educated students. Knowing he wanted to apply, we began checking off requirements: three SAT subject tests, parent essays, and an educational philosophy document. Not too long into the process, our son realized that applying was really not feasible in the time frame remaining. We abandoned the process. He was disappointed. I blamed myself for not doing more research, causing him not to have a chance to attend one of his top-choice schools. If only we had started the application process sooner. If only we had taken some SAT II subject tests just to be safe. I could have second guessed every decision we made along the way. My questioning would not have changed the circumstances. I could only see the temporary disappointment, not the big picture.

Six months later, as acceptance letters arrived in our mail box, our son processed the offers with some coaching. He knew exactly where he needed to be for the next four years. Six months had made a big difference in understanding. The decision had became clear, but not before having to wrestle with temporary setback and the character-building, relationship-growing conversations in which we engaged. We learned, grew, and moved forward toward the next chapter in life.

A Reason to Celebrate

We submitted our daughter's entire application package to the Air Force Academy by January 1 so she could be considered for early appointment. In February we were notified she was not chosen in this group, but was being passed on for the next board reviews.

According to what we've heard and read, most appointments are finalized by the end of March. Her JROTC instructor pulled her aside last week and said it's probably time for her to consider other options.

Cheryl, I'm sharing this with you because it, in a way, flies contrary to everything we try to teach about homeschooling in high school. I know the Academy is very accepting of homeschooled students and that she meets all of their requirements as an applicant. She legitimately earned all A's in what I taught her at home — her algebra tests don't lie. She was the top-scorer on all her JROTC assignments. She took Spanish with FLVS and aced those classes. She's received all A's in her dual-enrollment classes. She lettered in all four years of her sports, and is a state-ranked champion swimmer. She exceeded the minimum standards for physical ability and agility for entrance into the Academy. Her school counselor at the high school was thrilled to write a recommendation on her behalf, calling her a "unique, hybrid student who excels in ALL aspects of a varied educational experience." The school principal wrote her an outstanding recommendation and how as a part-time student she has had an enormous positive impact on the student body. I know at school, everyone expected she was a shoe-in for the Academy. At our JROTC awards banquet in January, she was asked to be the keynote speaker, introduced as the BEST Corp Commander by her leader, who called this the top rank achieved by a student that he has ever seen in all his years of working in JROTC.

As for the testing, I understand that she only scored a 28 on her ACT. We attribute that to not being "groomed" for test-taking as a homeschooler and her reading challenges; however, we sent her to several weeks of ACT-prep classes to help her learn the "tricks," and she took the ACT seven times to improve her score — if that doesn't prove tenacity, I don't know what does. In addition, I submitted all the documents to their standards. Every course description had the T's crossed and I's dotted perfectly.

I know God specializes in eleventh-hour miracles and that we cannot force the hand of God. Again, none of this makes any sense, Cheryl, except when it is put in perspective of God's perfect plan. Honestly, I am probably having a more difficult time accepting it than she is.

The next day...

Hey Cheryl, GOOD NEWS!!!

She was informed this morning she was accepted into the United States Air Force Academy.

Diplomas

"Will my home educated student receive a diploma?"

Another frequently asked question.

When homeschooling in the state of Florida, registered through a county home education program, the student will not be issued a diploma. The State for Florida cannot issue a high school diploma for a student who was not educated in a state public or registered private school. The home educating parent is the only agent who can issue a high school diploma to a student unless the student is enrolled in a correspondence program or private school.

Parents worry that employers will not hire and colleges will not accept a student without a high school diploma. These scenarios are rare. Home educated students are generally welcomed by employers and colleges because of their work ethic, character, and educational experiences. Today, employers and colleges realize a diploma is simply a piece of paper and not a guarantee of student or employee quality.

We know several homeschooled graduates aspiring to public service and safety, enrolling in either a police academy or fire school. These entities occasionally require additional paperwork or testing for entrance. One should research the requirements to be best prepared.

A Reason to Celebrate

Our young adult just graduated from firefighter training at the local state college. As a homeschooled graduate she had to take the TABE (Tests of Adult Basic Education), an academic assessment for adult education, for entrance into the program. The program did not accept financial aid. Finding out the entrance requirements for home educated students as well as the cost will save time and money when application time comes around. Our student had to work while attending, which was harder. The persistence — do not quit attitude — our young adult learned through homeschooling definitely provided preparation for the academy, which was difficult.

Students who enroll in community colleges, and some four-year universities, may be asked to take college placement exams. These tests are becoming increasingly popular in the areas of English, math, and science and are required whether or not a student graduates from a public or private school, homeschool, or holds a diploma.

Some families consider taking the General Education Development (GED) test, earning a passing score, and obtaining a diploma. Be sure to research this option completely. Though it may be a good idea for some circumstances, it may not be for others.

Affidavit for Completion of High School

In the state of Florida, students registered in **a** home education program graduate from home and do not earn a traditional, state-issued diploma. When I make this statement in my workshops, I see eyes open wide, followed by raised hands.

Most of us, being educated traditionally, have questions and concerns when thinking about our children not having a high school diploma. I did initially, until I understood why my home educated children would not be issued diplomas. Years later, with two home education graduates, neither having a diploma but both entering and graduating from post-secondary universities, I am not concerned. However, I do keep current with legislative changes. I further realize every student is unique in their postsecondary needs and my younger children may need a different path in their home education journey.

Home educated students do not earn a state diploma per Florida law, statute 1002.01, which defines a home education program as "sequentially progressive instruction of a student directed by his or her parent ." Because the home education program is directed by the parent, the state cannot evaluate the high school program of instruction; therefore, it cannot validate that the student earned a state-issued diploma. Hence, the only diploma that can be awarded is a diploma issued by the parents.

For admission to a state college, parents can sign and have notarized a home school affidavit testifying that the student completed a home education program according to the statute requirements. This document can be used in lieu of the state-issued diploma. In addition, the student may be required to take the PERT, SAT or ACT.

When applying to a state college, parents should research and be knowledgeable about this option. To illustrate, St. Petersburg College states one option for admission being a "home school affidavit signed by the student's parent/legal guardian attesting to the fact that the applicant has completed a home education program pursuant to the requirements of F.S. 1002.41, F.S." In another example, Seminole State College words their admission policy as such: "Students who have graduated from a home education program are eligible for admission as high school graduates. Students must provide a Seminole State College Affidavit of Home School Completion signed by a parent or legal guardian attesting that they have completed a home education program pursuant to the requirements in 1002.41 F.S. and provide their high school transcripts ." This information can be found at the following website:

🖥 https://www.seminolestate.edu/policiesprocedures/procedures/ studentinfo/3.0100

Finish Well

Gathering the final documents for employment or college admission is easier with proper, accurate record keeping. If records were not kept, start now, while there is time. With perseverance and determination, records can be written and paperwork organized. Be courageous. Get started. The finish line is within reach.

A Reason to Celebrate

Seven hours, two young adults, two parents, driving home. The topic of conversation? Economics. I promise you did not read that wrong. When there is a passion, it drives learning. My son has participated in competitive speech and debate for five years. His experiences with speech and debate have transformed his education by providing a purpose for his learning, by utilizing higher levels of thinking, and by producing a means by which information becomes applicable, not just memorized. Learning is authentic when a young adult must defend a case, which required hours of research, in front of judges. In the process, principles become applications with real world, personal impact. It is exciting and, it matters! He now engages in conversation, reflecting on what he has heard at competitions, breaking down the components of speeches, dissecting and analyzing what made them excellent. He has learned, first hand, the impact, power, and importance of words and is enthused about subjects he may not have given a second thought. There is a passion for knowledge and a wider understanding of the world. Why? He has had to develop cases on complex topics related to international and domestic policy and has had the opportunity to listen to others speak enthusiastically about topics. One of the topics was economics. His mind was stimulated and now he cannot stop talking about it, hence our car ride home.

I remember the beautiful fall day our oldest son Josh and I sat at the computer to print final documents—yes, before the days of uploading digital files. Full of anticipation, yet recollecting our days together, my fingers moved across the keyboard, making last minute edits. Finally, another file saved and then the printer hummed; pulling in paper and rolling it out. Josh placed each document on the stack, in the order specified on the application. The order, according to one college, was as important as the words penned on each page. Other colleges never specified order, just preferred specific documents. Following their specifications mattered.

Digital files now make submitting applications easier and much more efficient. There may not be a preferred order to the half-inch think stack of documents in an envelope, but there will be specific documents to email to particular individuals. Attention to details speaks to the work ethic of the student, making a good first impression. Be sure to double-check documents and follow the submission instructions provided by the college before hitting the send button.

We took the overstuffed envelopes to the post office, paid the postage and went home to wait. We were relieved, yet anxious. Would the homeschooled student stand out in the sea of applications? Would he get an unbiased review? Would the colleges requesting essays about our educational and grading philosophy be satisfied with the rigor of his work?

Two weeks later, Josh opened his first acceptance letter. Three weeks later another arrived. Several weeks after he received two more. In addition, two of the colleges offered an application to their honors colleges and two others offered Josh Presidential Scholarships, full-tuition for four years. Another letter offered a partial scholarship. Wow! We were elated. Hard work rewarded, we had finished with excellence.

A Reason to Celebrate

I have had to be my student's advocate. It is part of my role as her "guidance counselor". With her unique learning style and classes I researched college admission requirements for a university which was willing to think outside the box.

One of our obstacles forced me to ask questions. My daughter had completed specific courses at home which I knew were collage level. In fact, they were junior-senior major level. Knowing how hard my daughter worked, I felt compelled to ask the Dean if he would consider a personal interview and portfolio review in lieu of additional testing. He said they had never done such a thing but was willing to take our request into account. A phone call later in the week confirmed he saw the benefit of my inquiry.

I have learned important lessons while on my home education journey. First, champion your student. If you are certain he or she has qualifications, strengths, or an advanced knowledge in an area—and could validate such through a personal interview—seek that appointment and cheer him or her on through the process. Second, ask questions. Do not assume anyone has walked the same journey and knows the answers to your questions. Seek the information for yourself and research widely. I found out I could not sit around thinking I had situations figured out. Education and the job market are changing rapidly. In our planning with our students we learned we had to think ahead, five to six years out. Third, I learned I had to research my student's potential majors of interest, to see the end goal, and work back from there so we could choose our dual enrollment and college courses wisely. We did not want our student stuck with debt because we had exceeded the excess credit hour percentage.

There is so much for home education families to learn, yet so much potential. Every minute spent is worth the effort. Finishing well takes time and energy but the results are exceedingly delightful.

Cue *Pomp and Circumstance.* Send balloons aloft. Time to celebrate!

Celebrate the completion of what began the moment your child entered your home, in your arms, for the first time. Celebrate the accomplishments, the efforts, the time, and the energy put forth by student and parents, from grade school to high school graduation. Celebrate the people who poured into the life of the student—the parents, grandparents, mentors, the significant people who influenced and shaped the young adult. Celebrate the uniqueness of the individual, the heart, mind, and soul of the student.

As you walk through the last years of your student's high school journey, remember the final celebration is less about the knowledge stored up in student's mind and more about whether the young adult understands his or her strengths and how those strengths will bring value to whatever he or she endeavors. It is also about a young adult who is willing to take risks for the sake of other people or important causes. And, lastly the celebration is about a graduate with a willing, open heart, eager to make a difference, contributing to the community, the nation and the world.

That, dear friend, is something worth celebrating!

Notes

Made in the USA
San Bernardino, CA
11 July 2019